TREASURES OF
CHINA

TREASURES OF
CHINA

An Armchair Journey to over 340 Legendary Landmarks

Reader's Digest

Pleasantville, New York/Montreal

Contents

The Northern Region

The Great Wall 46-53

The Great Wall of the Warring Kingdoms • Jiayuguan • Watchtowers of the Great Wall • The Great Wall at Jinshan • Juyongguan • Bada Range • Shanhaiguan

The Western Region

The Silk Road **88-99**

Xi'an's City Wall • Mingsha Hills • Dafangpancheng • Jade Gate (Yumen-guan) • Ancient Altar (Gujitai) • The Mogao Grottoes • Crescent Moon Spring (Yueyaquan) • Polychrome Sculpture of Dunhuang • Murals at Mogao Grottoes • The Kizi Kuqa Beacon Tower • Bostan Lake • Bogda Peak • Ruins of Subashi

The Central Region (North)

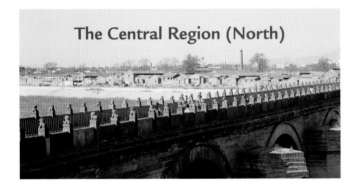

The Central Region (South)

The Southern Region

The Northern Region

 The rise of China as a distinct nation from a series of warring tribes is attributed to the power and aspiration of the rulers of the Qin (Chin) dynasty nearly 2200 years ago. The struggle for unity was momentous enough, but perhaps the most spectacular accomplishment was that of the first Qin emperor (Qinshihuangdi), who succeeded to the throne in 221 BC. To protect the infant nation from barbarian attack from the far north, he began work on that monumental and abiding symbol of Chinese civilization, the Great Wall, an immense Maginot Line of brick, packed mud and stone that was eventually to stretch some 3728 mi. (6000 km) across the Yellow River Valley and North China Plain to the Liaodong Peninsula.

It was a remarkable engineering feat and a colossal human achievement, with more than 500,000 peasant laborers pressed into work, but it also broke the back of the Qin rule. There was so much suffering and loss of life among the conscripts that, along with other painful and disruptive birth pangs of the new society, it led to the overthrow of the dynasty in 207 BC, four years after Qinshihuangdi's death.

Strictly speaking, this region refers to all areas north of the Great Wall, including the northeast and Inner Mongolia, as well as Chengde and Yinchuan. It is the cradle of the Manchus, the "barbarians" who eventually overran China in the 17th century and established what was to become the last of China's imperial dynasties. The region is bounded to the north, east and southeast by four main rivers—the Heilong, Wusuli, Tumen and Yalu—and within the territories that they form there are four principal mountain ranges: the Qian, Changbai, Da Xing'an (Hinggan) Ling and Xiao Xing'an (Hinggan) Ling.

Of these, Changbai sports the most dramatic scenery. Its main peak, Baitou, the tallest in the northeast, is capped with snow all year-round, and on its upper slopes lies the beautiful and moody Sky Lake (Tianchi)—a huge volcanic crater-lake surrounded by 16 precipitous mountain peaks, which can be beautifully serene one day and a maelstrom of high winds and crashing waves the next.

The Changbai Range is also the source of another important river of the northeast, the Songhua, the main tributary of the Heilong. Winding through some 60 percent of the territory, the Songhua feeds two of the most attractive cities of the area—Jilin, the "river city," famous for its frozen "tree hangings" in winter and its three nearby lakes, and Harbin, which is completely icebound throughout the long winter months. Harbin (its name is a corruption of a Jurchen phrase for "honor" and "great reputation") is celebrated for its beautiful Spring Festival, when the streets are lit at night with ice lanterns and ice and snow sculptures are displayed in its parks.

Shenyang, formerly Mukden, the capital of Liaoning Province, was once China's imperial capital—the founding emperor of the Manchu Qing dynasty (1644–1911) established his court there—and although the seat of rule was later returned to Beijing, the city has fared none the worse for it. Shenyang has continued to grow and prosper, and is endowed with imperial architecture—the Imperial Palace, imperial mausoleums of Taizu and Taizong, and some 70 other courts and administrative buildings—which is among the most extensive and best preserved in China and ranks with the Forbidden City in Beijing.

By contrast, the western area of the northeast, beyond the Da Xing'an Range, is a seemingly boundless prairie dotted here and there with dense forests—the Mongolian tableland. Lying about 3281 ft. (1000 m) above sea level, this is a land of sweeping plains, fierce summer and winter temperatures and nomadic Mongolian "cowboys," who live in felt tents, follow Tibetan lamaism, ride swift ponies and tend sheep, goats and cattle—"The sky so blue, the field so vast," as an old Chinese poem describes it, "When the wind blows the grass bows low, baring the sheep and cattle below."

With all this grassland it is not surprising that the capital city of Inner Mongolia, Huhehaote (Huhhot), is known as the "green city." It is also a treasure house of Tibetan Buddhist architecture, featuring several lamaseries, or monasteries, filled with finely executed sculptures, murals and frescoes.

Mohe

漠河

This, the northernmost outpost of China, is called the Arctic City because of its bitterly cold winter climate. Its people call it the town of the White Night for the time of the annual summer solstice, when darkness closes in for only an hour or two before and after midnight. But its most dramatic feature is its natural *son et lumière* of the aurora borealis, the northern lights, when a small ring of light appears to the north of the city, expands until it literally fills the sky with color, then retreats and disappears to the east.

◀

WUSULI RIVER
烏蘇里江

One of the major tributaries of the Heilong, the Wusuli River is a strategic one, for it serves as a boundary between China and Russia. It is also one of the coldest places in China, with temperatures often plunging to -22°F (-30°C) in winter.

This river measures 553 mi. (890 km) in length and flows through an area of 73,340 sq. mi. (190,000 sq. km) of fertile virgin forests, mineral resources and agricultural products such as soybeans and sorghum.

Zhenbao is a blunt finger of land 1.2 mi. (2 km) long, jutting out from the Chinese side of the Wusuli. Eroded by the river water, the connecting strip of land has been submerged. Thus Zhenbao becomes an island when the river is high. However, land emerges during the dry summer season when the water level is low, connecting it once again to the mainland. It is an important fishing center, and even in the coldest months, when the Wusuli is frozen over, lines are cast Eskimo-style through the ice. In the autumn the river abounds with sturgeon and maha that are sometimes 13 to 16 ft. (4 to 5 m) in length, weigh 1543 to 1764 lb. (700 to 800 kg) and have been known to gather in such staggering numbers to spawn that, as the *Heilongjiang Gazette* has observed, "their density was so great that local people would occasionally walk on them to cross the river." ▲

FIVE CONNECTED LAKES
五大連池

Between 1719 and 1721, huge volcanic eruptions tore through the mountains in the upper reaches of the River Bai, about 14 mi. (22 km) north of Dedu County in Heilongjiang Province. Masses of lava flooded and crashed into the river, damming it and forming one of China's most dramatic scenic spots, the Five Connected Lakes. From the vantage point of one of the mountains, Laohei, these lakes tumble through the craggy folds of the landscape like a string of blue gems. Surrounding them are no less than 24 active volcanoes, some of them smoothed away by the elements and others with distinctive cone-shaped peaks. This Museum of Volcanoes, as it is known, has long been a popular hot springs resort. Not only did the lava flows create the lakes, they also divided the lower reaches of the River Bai into two streams—the Shilong He (Stone Dragon River) to the east and, to the west, the Yaoquan He, or Medicinal Spring River.

On another local mountain, Huoshao, the lava flows not only cooled into a natural monstrosity of charred rocks and huge fissures but carried on to form a "stone dragon" sprawling for a couple of kilometers or miles across the adjacent hills. Viewed from a distance, this "dragon" looks more like a turbulent river, its waters caught and frozen in a split second of time. But at close range, the lava has settled and twisted into weird shapes that resemble tigers, elephants, horses and giant lizards. The Five Connected Lakes is now one of the eight Chinese geoparks. ▼

DONGZHENG CHURCH
東正教堂

Russian priests established the Dongzheng (Eastern Orthodox) Church in Harbin in 1899—a magnificent domed Byzantine structure and the finest of some 17 churches that they eventually built in the northeast. It still stands today, a reminder of the tumultuous struggles of the past and a witness to that most crucial of all struggles in Chinese history—the extent to which the Chinese have been willing to tolerate outside influence. Western religion and all foreign thought were rejected entirely during the violent cultural revolution of the late 1960s. Now, in its dramatic swing toward modernization and technological competition with the West, China's doors are open again, and a degree of religious freedom is permitted. But so too is a far more marked, and perhaps premeditated, tolerance of Confucianism—the abiding ethic of Chinese society—and it would be reckless indeed to predict that places of worship such as Harbin's Dongzheng Church will remain much more than an architectural relic. ▼

TAIYANG DAO
太陽島

The Taiyang Dao, or Sun Island, is a 4-sq. mi. (10-sq. km) shoal on the Songhua River in Harbin, neatly landscaped with parklands, flowering shrubs and trees to serve as the city's main summer resort. With its spacious gardens and riverside groves of willow trees, it adds luster to Harbin's long-standing reputation as the "jade" mounted on the shimmering silver necklace of the Songhua. ◀ ▼

Jingbo Lake
鏡泊湖

Jingbo Lake is another popular, though far more magnificent, northeastern resort—the largest dammed lake in China. Situated 31 mi. (50 km) southwest of Ning'an County in Heilongjiang on the upper reaches of the Mudan (Peony) River, it is 28 mi. (45 km) long and 4 mi. (6 km) wide and covers an area of 35 sq. mi. (90 sq. km). Its banks lie under high peaks and craggy walls, some of which hang in sheer precipices over the water.

These cliffs, peaks and scenic spots provide a number of spectacular viewpoints, which are called the Eight Sights of Jingbo—the Great Gu Mountain, Little Gu Mountain, Baishilazi, Laoguanlazi, Zhenzhumen, Chengqianglazi, Daoshi Mountain and the Diaoshuilou Waterfall. ▲

Xingkai Lake
興凱湖

Lying on the border between northeastern China and Russia, the Xingkai Lake actually forms the boundary between the two countries. In a treaty signed in 1860 between Beijing and Moscow, a line was drawn midway between the north and the south, and today more than half of the lake's area lies in Russia. The lake was formed when the land here subsided after a volcanic eruption. Xingkai in Manchurian means "water flowing down from higher grounds." The lake is 226 ft. (69 m) above sea level and has an area of 1691 sq. mi. (4380 sq. km), some of which are 33 ft. (10 m) deep. Nine rivers flow into it before it empties itself into the Wusuli River in the northeast. A smaller lake, called Little Xingkai, is linked to the large lake during flood time. The former lies entirely within Chinese territory. Xingkai Lake was called Meituo Lake during the Tang dynasty, named after the fish that flourished there. Nowadays, many different species of freshwater fish continue to be harvested, including sturgeon and freshwater porpoise. During the cold season, the lake freezes into a vast expanse of snow-brushed ice. ▼

SONGHUA RIVER
松花江

This mighty river is typical of much of the majesty of the northeast—no less than 1143 mi. (1840 km) long and flowing through more than 193,000 sq. mi. (500,000 sq. km) of largely untamed land. Yet it is actually only a tributary, albeit the largest, of an even bigger river, the Heilong. And it has a benign and even touching aspect to its character: In the wintertime, when the temperature can drop to as low as –22°F(–30°C) and the river is icebound for up to five months at a time, a section of its waters around the Fengman Hydroelectric Power Station near Jilin remains free of ice, warmed by heated waste from the plant. Vapor rises from the river surface, condenses, then settles and freezes on the branches of willow trees that line the bank for miles. The result is an exquisite fairyland effect that the Chinese call "shu gua," or tree hangings,

and which the more poetic have hailed "jade trees with silver branches." Since the time of the Qing dynasty, ice lanterns have been a popular folk art of the area, hung under the snowpacked eaves of homes and sometimes lit with candles.

Elsewhere, and on the more mundane level, the Songhua flows through the most extensive and possibly richest of China's wildernesses. It contains untouched forests that may yield lumber amounting to several billion cubic yards or meters. Coal, gold, copper, iron and other minerals abound. The Songhua's fertile river basin produces soybeans, corn, sorghum, cotton, tobacco and orchard fruits, and the river is also rich in freshwater fish, particularly carp, of which around 88 million lb. (40 million kg) are caught each year. ▲

SONGHUA LAKE
松花湖

Lying on the upper reaches of one of the two main tributaries that feed the Songhua River is Songhua Lake, a popular tourist spot whose waters are dotted with dinghies and sailboats in the summer and whose icy surface swishes with sleighs and skates in the winter season. As with most of the lakes of the northeast, Songhua Lake is surrounded by mountain peaks and forests and its shoreline is pitted with quiet and secluded bays and beaches. It also has its own islet, Wuhu, or Five Tigers, which is a favorite fishing spot for the locals.

But for all its beauty, Songhua Lake is also a strategic part of the industrial infrastructure of the northeast. It is a vast reservoir, almost inland sea, with its waters stretching some 124 mi. (200 km) to the boundary of Huadian County, and it feeds the Fengman Hydroelectric Power Station, which was built during the Japanese occupation. It is also well stocked with freshwater fish and provides irrigation to surrounding croplands. ▼

WUSONG ISLAND
霧淞島

When winter arrives, a couple of small island villages near the City of Jilin offer the best place to view icicles, called Wusong or Shu Gua in Chinese. The two quiet villages, mostly populated by the Man ethnic minority, draw tens of thousands of people every winter to admire the beauty of nature's winter creations and to enjoy the ethnic culture of the Man. Although the power plant and recent development in Jilin has spoiled typical icicle-viewing places in the city, these two villages, known as Wusong Island, still attract hardy winter tourists to this well-named Ice and Snow Shangrila, so surreal that visitors feel they are in a frozen fairyland. ▶

MANCHUGUO PALACE
偽滿皇宮

Of all the foreign challenges and incursions suffered by China, none is regarded as more savage and infamous than that of the Japanese occupation of the early 1930s. Emboldened by their stunning naval triumph over the Russians in 1904–5, their occupation of Taiwan and annexation of Korea, the Japanese invaded Manchuria in 1931. They then booted out the remnants of Russian influence and established a puppet government of Manchuguo (Manchukuo) under the last, deposed emperor of China, Henry Pu Yi. Here, visitors can see where he banqueted foreign diplomats and received the real power behind the Manchuguo throne, the commander-in-chief of the Japanese Guandong army. ▷

JILIN CATHEDRAL
吉林教堂

Roman Catholicism was first introduced into China in 1508 at the waning end of the "glorious" Ming dynasty, and it appeared to have perhaps the best hope of all foreign religions of taking root and flourishing in the hitherto Buddhist Middle Kingdom.

Though suppressed in China during the 18th and early 19th centuries, Catholicism nevertheless survived, and in 1838 it was able to find root in the northeast, where great places of worship, such as the Jilin Cathedral, were built. Many of them, like this cathedral, were an almost perfect transplant of European Gothic architecture. In 1838, with the British and European navies and armed merchantmen forcing the Qing dynasty to its knees, an independent diocese was established in the region under Bishop Fang Ruowang, and it lasted for more than 30 years. In 1905, the Jilin Diocese was placed under the supervision of the French. ◁

CHANGBAI MOUNTAIN
長白山

This huge volcanic mountain range, stretching from southeast Jilin Province to the northern part of the Korean Peninsula, is one of the great natural treasures of China. It is rich in beauty, abounds with exotic wildlife and is a major source of ingredients for one of the most complex and most valued institutions of Chinese culture—herbal medicine. Chinese historians attribute the birth of Chinese medicine to a legendary emperor, Shen Nong, who is said to have reigned some 5000 years ago and to have become fascinated by the apparent medicinal properties of various plants. "Shen Nong tested the myriad

herbs," wrote the Han dynasty historian Sima Qian (Ssu-ma Chien), "and so the art of medicine was born." That art has developed over the centuries into an immense pharmacopoeia of potions, pills, salves, tonics and other remedies taken from plants or from animals and reptiles.

Changbai Mountain was once an active volcano, and although it has erupted twice in relatively modern times—in the 17th and 18th centuries—it is now regarded as dormant. It features a group of 72 lakes which are formed from volcanic craters, the largest being the spectacular Sky Lake (or Tianchi in Chinese). ▲

Sea of Forests (Linhai)

The Chinese reverence for nature and myth is reflected in the pictures they have painted of forests that rear up and roll and swell, and the leafy waves that lift and crest for as far as the eye can see around the beautifully named Sky Lake, in the heart of the Changbai Mountain Range. The forests sweep to the east, west and north of the lake in Antu, Fusong and Changbai counties and cover a total area of about 1544 sq. mi. (4000 sq. km). Their character and category change according to the altitude: Up to 3280 ft. (1000 m) the trees are largely leaf-shedding pines, willow and birch; at 3280 to 5900 ft. (1000 to 1800 m) lies the needle birch zone and the slopes are thick with evergreen pines and firs; at the highest altitude, the Yuehualin zone at 5900 to 6560 ft. (1800 to 2000 m), the steep gradients and cold, windy conditions have made the tree cover more stunted and sparse. ◂

Sky Lake (Tianchi)

Millions of years ago the Changbai Mountain (Snow-capped Mountains) thundered and rocked with almost continuous volcanic eruptions. The legacy of that prehistoric violence is a series of 60 deep craters that have since filled with water to form the beautiful and brooding Sky Lake, south of Baihe County in Jilin Province. It is one of the world's most magnificent sights, lying just over 6560 ft. (2000 m) above sea level, covering an area of 3.55 sq. mi. (9.2 sq. km). Its waters are more than 984 ft. (300 m) deep in some places and surrounded by 16 mountain peaks.

In fine weather, the lake is so serene and its waters so clear that you can see the rocks many fathoms down on its bed. But the weather can change very abruptly, and strong winds can whip the face of the lake into a rage of 3-ft.(1-m) high waves. In the winter months, the mood changes again, the frozen surface mirroring the mountain peaks around it.

THOUSAND MOUNTAINS (QIAN SHAN)
千山

Located east of Anshan in Liaoning Province, the Qian is a range of almost a thousand mountain peaks. In ancient times it was called Thousand Lotus Blossoms Mountain because the peaks were seen as a vast cluster of lotus blooms on a pond, and not surprisingly, its dramatic beauty and isolation have made it a holy place, revered in poetry and song:

If you do not ascend the Immortal's Terrace,
Your visit to Qian Mountains is wasted.
Once you are on top of the Immortal's Terrace,
You can see the Bo Sea in the east.

Indeed, the Immortal's Terrace is the highest spot, 2323 ft. (708 m) to its peak, where the characters Xian Ren Tai, carved into a huge rock, proclaim its name. On the second highest peak, Wufo, five stone Buddha images await those of the faithful who can complete the grueling climb. The guide to Thousand Mountains lists no less than 164 places of interest, including many Buddhist and Taoist monasteries and temples. Some of the most striking ones were built in the early part of the Manchu Qing dynasty—the largest of them, the Wuliang Monastery, featuring ornate shrines to the gods. ▲ ▶

ZHAO TOMBS
昭陵

The Manchu dynasty, which ruled China from 1644 until the republican revolution of 1911, seized power from the waning Mings with a fierce military alliance of peoples from "beyond the Great Wall." Yet the name Manchu did not really come into being until the imperial throne had been taken, and the dynasty itself represented the triumph of a war machine created by a mixture of Mongol pastoralists, urban traders, hunters and fishermen welded together in the 17th century by a chieftain of the primitive Tungu tribe. Once in power, this Manchu culture was rapidly diluted and assimilated by the predominant Han or Chinese culture of the south.

Zhao Tombs, also known as North Tombs (Bei Ling), stand in the city of Shenyang as a memorial to the military success of the Manchus. It is the tomb of the Manchu warlord Taizong, who led the "barbarian" alliance to the very foot of the imperial throne. Construction of the tomb began in 1643, the year before the Manchus took power, and it was completed in 1651. It was extended into an imperial mausoleum during the reigns of Taizong's successors, the emperors Shunzhi (1644–1661), Qianlong (1736–1796) and Jiaqing (1796–1820).

Surrounded by massive stone walls, the entire burial complex covers 1,936,800 sq. ft. (180,000 sq. m) and includes finely carved arches, ornamental pillars, stone lions, bridges, ceremonial pavilions and the magnificent Longen shrine hall, with its ornately carved colonnades and yellow-glazed tile roof. ▲ ▼

Fu Tombs

福陵

Another Manchu emperor, Taizu, was buried with his queen in the Fu Tombs, also called East Tombs for its location in the eastern suburbs of Shenyang. Started in 1629 and completed in the same year as Taizong's tomb, they lie on the thickly wooded bank of the Hun River with the Tianzhu Mountain behind them.

Though the tombs' architecture and layout are quite different from Taizong's resting place, they include the usual arches, bridges, ceremonial pavilions and carved animals—and the divine touch of the Manchu emperors.

The building complex faces south and is surrounded by massive walls. In the middle of the south wall is the main gate, which is flanked by glazed tiles decorated with a dragon motif.

On both sides of the open porch of the main gate there are *Xiama*, or "alight from horse," tablets that are found in most imperial burial places. "All officials below the rank of prince should dismount here," they warn. The Xiama at this tomb were originally inscriptions in wood, but these were replaced with stone in 1783 when emperor Qianlong visited the tombs to pay his respects.

The pailou or main arch (top, opposite), has a double-eaved roof covered by yellow glazed tiles. Beyond the arch stands a stela, or stone pillar. The inscription on it is a eulogy to the greatness of the imperial ancestors in the calligraphy of emperor Kangxi.

In layout design, Fu Tombs are similar to Zhao Tombs, with the same names for its structures and buildings, although a bit smaller in size. The fortresslike building complex behind the pailou is called a courtyard, or "fang chen," which is encircled with brick walls, forming the center of the tombs. The main gate is called Longen Men or "sacrificial gate" (opposite bottom).

On a platform in the middle of the walled fang chen stands the Longen Shrine Hall, or "sacrificial hall" (picture below).

THE ANCIENT PALACE (SHENYANG)

瀋陽故宮

Though the Tungu tribal chieftain, Nuerhachi, is said to have first gathered together the Manchu military alliance, the warlord Huang Taiji is credited with the first major step toward what was envisioned as Manchu nationhood and empire. It was he, the records say, who conquered and united the entire northeast, and for this he was installed as king in Chongzheng Hall, one of more than 70 great pavilions and courts in the Ancient Palace in Shenyang. In scale and architecture this palace rivals the Forbidden City in Beijing. Construction began in 1625 and was completed in 1636, and to any visitor from the south, it must have stood as a mighty portent of the imperial conquest that was to come. It became the seat of power of all the early Manchu kings—Taizong and Taizu among them—and was renovated and extended by the emperors Kangxi and Qianglong in the succeeding era of imperial triumph.

Built in three sections, each of them containing separate courts with their own halls, shrines and pavilions, the palace features the beautiful three-story Fenghuang (Phoenix) Mansion, a royal banquet hall whose top floor offers a panoramic view of modern Shenyang. Another mansion, Wensu, houses two voluminous and academically invaluable anthologies of Manchu history. ▲

Dazheng Hall and Shiwang Pavilions

The Dazheng Hall and Shiwang Pavilions form the east section of the Ancient Palace and, more than anything else, commemorate the militaristic nature of the Manchus. The Dazheng Hall, an eight-sided double-eaved wooden structure crowned with a golden dragon, has a row of five pavilions on each side of it, extending from north to south, each built of blue-green bricks and supported by red pillars. The effect is very much like two lines of army tents guarding the commander-in-chief—a symbol of the success of the Qing dynasty's founder, emperor Shunzhi, who spent the better part of his life on the battlefield and was blessed with the loyal support of his generals.

The Shiwang Pavilions is where the 10 most important lieutenants of the Manchu king—two princes and eight ministers—met each day to plan the campaign of military strategy and political intrigue that was aimed at imperial rule. The complex, actually a series of interconnected rooms, is now a museum of Manchu armor, carriages, military costume, campaign banners and weapons, including a sword that is said to have been worn by emperor Qianlong and is still untarnished today, more than two centuries after his reign. ▼ ▶

XILITU TEMPLE

席力圖召

The Xilitu Temple, situated in the old wall of Huhehaote (Hohhot), was built in the Ming dynasty but enlarged over the years until, in the early Qing reign, it included a shrine hall with eight columns. When emperor Kangxi returned from a military expedition to the Western frontiers, he visited the temple, bestowed gifts of sutras, rosaries and weapons and gave it a Han name, the Yanshou Monastery. A tablet commemorating his victory is still standing in an eight-cornered pavilion, inscribed with details of his battles in Han, Manchu, Mongolian and Tibetan. As with most monasteries in the northeast, the architecture is principally Chinese, with the main shrine hall and sutra hall in the Tibetan style. ◄

Dajingtang

This, the principal building or Great Sutra Hall of the Xilitu Temple, has walls inlaid with peacock-blue tiles adorned with gilded silver decorations. The roof is more ornate, mounted with a gilded vase (baoping), Tibetan prayer wheel, a flying dragon and a deer—all cast in copper and contrasting with the red door and polychrome painting below. Eight Tibetan columns support the front porch. The two-story building is where the lamas gather to chant the Buddhist scriptures. ▼

SHELI PAGODA
金剛座舍利寶塔

Buddhism spread to China from India in the 1st century AD and faced a society that not only boasted an already long-established civilization but considered itself the only truly civilized society on earth. It took a long and arduous struggle for the new belief to take root, and even then it survived largely because it was able to adapt to and complement China's traditional native teachings—Confucianism and Taoism—rather than attempting to usurp them. The Chinese are thought to have first come into contact with Buddhism through central Asians traveling in from the north and northwest. Later, between the 7th and 10th centuries, it literally flooded in, along with other religions and sects from the West across the deserts, mountains and steppes of that fabled Central Asian trade route, the Silk Road. And alongside these other religions, it eventually came under the hammer of an imperial edict, issued in AD 845, declaring that all imported foreign influence had gone far enough.

But while chastened, Buddhism has survived, and in China's northeast there are many fine temples, such as the Jingangzuo Sheli Pagoda, near the old wall of Huhehaote (Hohhot) in Inner Mongolia, which were built as late as the Qing dynasty and exhibit a mixture of Han, Mongol and Tibetan Buddhist influences typical of this frontier region. Sheli Pagoda is the only section of the much larger Cideng (popularly known as Five Tower) Monastery that has managed to withstand the ravages of time. It consists of five square-shaped brick-and-stone towers, faced with glazed tiles and, mounted upon a stone base—an example of a particularly rare form of Buddhist architecture. ▲

WUDANG TEMPLE
五當召

Another grand example of Tibetan Buddhist architecture, the Wudang Lamasery, lies on a mountain slope 43 mi. (70 km) northwest of Baotou, the biggest city in Inner Mongolia. It is the only surviving complete lamasery in the region, with more than 2500 living units, classrooms, temples and halls of worship, and is one of the main centers of lamaism in China. Built in 1749 by the Dalai lama himself, its name in Mongolian means "willow tree." The temple is built in the traditional Tibetan style, with monolithic white stone walls, but this rather forbidding simplicity gives way to striking color inside the temples and schools. In the main hall, Suguqindu, for example, where the lamas gather to conduct prayers and perform the chanting of the scriptures, the columns are clad in colorfully woven pillar rugs. The floors are similarly carpeted, and religious murals cover the walls. The two floors above the hall are filled with images of Sakyamuni and other Buddhist deities. In another hall, Queyilindu, the center for the teaching of the sutras, there is a bronze Sakyamuni figure 33 ft. (10 m) tall.

Other halls in the sprawling complex are schools for the teaching of medicine, astronomy and geography, and the history and disciplines of lamaism. There is also a museum of sorts, the Dongkuoerdu Hall, displaying relics and personal effects left by seven Dalai Lamas who were in temporary residence here at various times in the past. ▲

MONGOL TEMPLE
蒙古廟

Although a distinctive school of Buddhism centered on the palace of the Dalai Lama in Lhasa, Tibetan Lamaism is also widespread in Mongolia and Manchuria. In Inner Mongolia, lamaseries dot the sparsely inhabited grasslands, most of them a blend of Tibetan and Han Chinese architectural styles. Two fine examples are Wusutu Temple and Xilitu Temple, erected during the Ming Dynasty and still remarkably well preserved after a series of renovations. Temples built during the later Qing rule include those at Meidai, Bailing and Beizi. ▶

HUAYAN SUTRA PAGODA
萬部華嚴經塔

Located in the eastern section of Huhehaote City, the Huayan Sutra Pagoda goes by the far more formidable full name of Wanbu Huayan Jingta (Ten Thousand Volumes of Avata-masake Sutra Pagoda), but it is commonly called the White Tower. It is also a fine example of earlier Buddhist architecture, probably erected between AD 983 and 1031 in the era of Song refinement and enlightenment that followed the Tang dynasty's crackdown on "alien" religions. It is an eight-sided tower of wood and brick, seven storys or 148 ft. (45 m) high—imposing even for the inspirational architecture of its time. It stands upon the site of what was formerly a monastery named Daxuanjiao, and within its walls there is a remarkable display of historical graffiti—inscribed by various visitors as far back as the Jin dynasty (1115–1234) and written not only in Chinese but also Mongolian, Nuzhen, ancient Syrian and Persian. ◀

THE MAUSOLEUM OF GENGHIS KHAN
成吉思汗陵

Genghis Khan, meaning "emperor of all emperors,' or "universal ruler," is regarded by many as the greatest conqueror of all time in terms of the number of square miles or kilometers he conquered. At the time of his sudden death at the age of 65 in 1227, caused by a fall from his horse while leading the fight against the Tangut, he had laid the foundation for an empire that was going to stretch from Hungary to Korea, almost two thirds of the known world.

Genghis Khan was born in 1167 and was named Temujen after a Tatar chieftain his father, himself a Kiyat tribe chieftain, had captured. According to legend, he was an adept fighter at a young age, known for his brilliant military strategy. In 1206, after unifying the Mongols, he was acknowledged as the supreme leader of the steppes of Asia.

No one knows exactly where the supreme ruler was buried, but the monument to Genghis Khan is located in the Ordos region of Inner Mongolia. It is said that during his last military campaign the great Khan expressed a desire to be buried in the beautiful Ordos greasslands. Originally, 500 families, called the Darkhad Mongols, were chosen by the family of Genghis Khan to preserve and carry on the memorial ceremonies since the 13th cen-tury, from the regular ceremonies that were held twice a month to major festivals held two or three times a year, culminating in the great festival when Mongol noblemen from all parts of Mongolia would gather and participate in the ceremonies. ▲

ZHAOJUN'S TOMB
昭君墓

The tomb of Wang Zhaojun, a 108-ft. (33-m) high mound of loess (sandstone), stands on the south bank of the Dahei River about 6 mi. (9 km) south of Huhehaote.

The story of Wang Zhaojun has twisted and changed over the centuries but can be traced back to the tale of Wang Zhaojun, a girl from a good family, who was selected to live in the Han imperial court. A prince named Huhanye from the Xiongnu region came to visit the court and expressed his desire to marry the girl for the sake of closer ties with the imperial throne. In local legends, Zhaojun was regarded not only as a guardian angel for thriving animal husbandry, but also endowed with the power to cure infertility in women. Although it is the burial place of an imperial concubine, the people of the Huhehaote region believe that a pinch of soil taken from the grass-covered tomb will make childless women pregnant. ▶

DAZHAO MONASTERY

大召

The Dazhao Monastery in the old section of Huhehaote presents a different architectural picture of Chinese Lamaism, a blend of Chinese and Tibetan Buddhist design. Built in the Chinese style in 1580, it was extended during the reign of the Qing emperor Kangxi, and the roof of the main shrine hall was clad with yellow-glazed tiles. However, the main structure of the hall is distinctly Tibetan, a traditional double-story white fortress design with a porch, sutra chamber and a Buddha shrine, where the most valued possession of the lamasery is on display—an image of Sakyamuni cast entirely in silver. It is from this splendid statue that the lamasery takes its popular Chinese name, Silver Buddha Monastery. ◀

THE MONGOLIAN PASTURES
草原牧場

For panorama, there is little to compare with the eastern expanses of the Inner Mongolian tableland. It is a flat green sea of pastureland stretching across the horizon, broken only by an occasional cluster of sheep and cattle and yurts—the portable felt igloo-shaped tents of the nomads—and their wraiths of cooking smoke.

These Mongolian "cowboys," about one and a half million of whom live in Inner Mongolia, make their livelihood from breeding and raising flocks of sheep and goats and herds of cattle, horses and camels. These expert horsemen are ruddy, strong-faced people, with high cheekbones and distinctive straight noses.

There is evidence on this boundless pasture of the fear that these once-unconquerable mounted warriors struck into the hearts of their immediate neighbors and the Han Chinese to the south—two ancient walls, built by the Nuzhens, the ancestors of the Manchus, probably to guard against Mongol attacks. Both are more than 62 mi. (100 km) long. One lies to the northwest of the region along the Ergun River to the west bank of the Lai Lake, and the other is in the southeast, running from the southern slopes of the Daxing'an Ling Range to Solon. ▲ ▼

HAI PAGODA
海寶塔

One of the oldest and most interesting Buddhist structures in the northeast is the Hai Pagoda, or North Pagoda, in the city of Yinchuan. Although there is no actual record of the date of construction, a book written in the Ming reign says it was rebuilt in the 5th century by a local prince. There are later records, however, of its renovation after an earthquake between the reigns of the Qing emperors Kangxi and Qianlong.

Standing on a high and spacious square base, the pagoda is built entirely of brick and rises 11 stories to a height of 177 ft. (54 m). It has an unusual design: A broad ridge rises from the middle of each wall, occupying one third of the wall surface, so that each of its four walls looks as though it is actually three. Viewed from a distance, this design creates an optical illusion in which the pagoda has 12 corners and 12 high windows shaped like Buddha niches. The structural lines are well defined, giving the building an austere and robust character. Its roof is a peach-shaped dome of green tiles. ◀

Imperial Summer Villa
避暑山莊

The Imperial Summer Villa in Chengde, the biggest garden palace complex in China, was started in 1703 and took 87 years to complete. It was a summer resort for the Manchu Qing emperors and was also known as the Jehol Traveling Lodge or Li Palace. Its grounds, only 20 percent of which are lakes and gardens, and the rest hills, are guarded by a wall that runs 6.2 mi. (10 km) around the perimeter.

The villa itself includes the Central Palace, Pine-and-Crane Studio, East Palace and a residential complex known as Wanhesongfeng. As with all Chinese courts, the architecture is elegant with one aim in mind: to promote peace and harmony. Bronze lions guard the outer gate, and the main door to the compound proclaims its name in characters that are said to have been inscribed by emperor Kangxi himself. Visitors can view the Danpojingcheng ceremonial hall, built of wood from the nanmu tree, the emperor's bedchamber and a two-story mansion in which the stairs form part of an artificial hill of rock. The decor of the entire palace complex is pleasantly free of ornate carvings, gilt or decorative painting—a purely rustic refuge from the summer dust storms and political heat of court life in Beijing.

Misty Rain Mansion

As its name suggests, this mansion was specially designed for the enjoyment of mist and rain on the surrounding lakes and hills. Standing on the rise of Great Lotus Island, it was styled after a mansion of the same name on Mandarin Duck Island in South Lake, Zhejiang. It is a two-story single-eaved building supported by red pillars and clad with green glazed tiles. Its name was bestowed by emperor Kangxi, and it is inscribed in his own hand on a plaque on the upper floor.

The mansion's east side includes a three-room study, which was the emperor's book house, or reading room. The western section is called the Facing Hills Studio. Pavilions stand on three sides of the building, and the view includes the Ten-Thousand-Trees Garden, the Jehol Springs and Yongyou Monastery. The mansion and its gardens are at their best in the summer months when the lotuses are in bloom, the rain settles in a gossamer mist on the leafy pools and a smoky mist rises from the waters. ▶

Zhijingyun Dyke

The Manchu emperor Kangxi, who reigned from 1662 to 1723, was not only a staunch military defender of the realm but a man of certain culture and refinement. And when the Manchu rulers built their magnificent Imperial Summer Villa in Chengde, much of Kangxi's artistic vision went into it. The Zhijingyun Dyke, a vast and beautiful series of pools and water gardens modeled on the West Lake of Hangzhou, was laid in one of 36 scenic spots selected by the emperor himself. This charming blend of man-made ponds, dykes, islands and willow-lined promenades became the jewel in the crown of a palace garden covering no less than 53.8 million sq. ft. (5 million sq. m)—double the area of the Summer Palace in Beijing. The Chinese love of nature and their respect for what they see as the natural harmony of existence is reflected in the names they gave their gardens and pavilions. North of the Zhijingyun Dyke there lies, for example, the Misty Rain Mansion. ◄

Heavy-Snow-on-South-Hill Pavilion

The Heavy-Snow-on-South-Hill Pavilion stands on a hilltop in the northwest section of the gardens along with three other evocatively named buildings on other hilltops close by: Surrounded-by-Hills-and-Clouds Pavilion, Two-North-Peaks-as-Pillows Pavilion and the Pointed-Peak-Setting-Sun Pavilion. The square Heavy-Snow Pavilion, with its winged tentlike roof, was given its name by Kangxi and stands rather precariously on the edge of a bluff. The view from there is outstanding. ◄

Shuixin (Lake Center) Pavilion

This pavilion, lying north of the main palace area and south of Misty Rain Mansion, was once the watergate on the border of the lakes. In 1709, during extensive redevelopment of the summer villa grounds, the Silver Lake and Mirror Lake were added to the eastern fringe, along with three pavilions that emperor Kangxi named collectively Lake Center Pavilion. All three structures stand on bridges into which as many as eight watergates have been set. ▼

Putuo Zongcheng Temple

Built in 1767, this lamasery is designed in a series of terraced steps up a broad hillside and is modeled on the seat of Tibetan Buddhism, the Potala Palace in Lhasa. It consists of some 40 buildings—shrines and dormitories for the monks—dominated from the crest of the hill by the monolithic Red Terrace, which houses the principal Wanfaguiyi Shrine. This huge structure is built on granite foundations, rises 141 ft. (43 m) high and has walls of pink and white stone. Its tapered roof, covered with copper fish-scale tiles, is one of the finest examples of Tibetan Buddhist architecture outside Tibet itself. ▲

The Thousand Hands and Thousand Eyes Bodhisattva

This statue, one of the biggest wooden Buddha images in the world, stands more than 72 ft. (22 m) high and is constructed of five different timbers: elm, fir, pine, juniper and cypress. More than three tons of metal were used to link and reinforce its torso and many limbs. The head alone weighs five and a half tons, and the weight of the entire image is estimated at a little under 125 tons. The statue has 42 arms, with each hand holding a sacred object and each palm containing an eye. The face has three eyes, symbolizing the Buddha's ability to know the past, present and future. As a Bodhisattva, the image also represents a being whose essence has achieved wisdom but whose fate is to undergo many rebirths, existing for the good and guidance of others, until eventually reaching Buddhahood. Above this image stands a 5-ft. (1.4-m) high Amitabha Buddha (not seen in this picture), also known as the Impersonal Buddha and believed to preside over the Paradise of the West, where the souls of the pious go to exist in a state of bliss. ◄

Puning Temple

An enormous, ornately decorated wooden Buddha dominates the main hall of the Puning Temple, built in 1755 to the northeast of the Imperial Summer Villa. It was commissioned and installed to commemorate a Qing dynasty victory over rebellious Mongols supported by the Russians. A detailed account of the battle, the Conquest of Tian Mountain, is inscribed on stone tablets in Chinese, Mongolian, Manchurian and Tibetan in an adjacent yellow-tiled pavilion. Two other shrines feature an image of the Maitreya Buddha, or Future Buddha, and Sakyamuni, the Indian prince who, seeking to be emancipated from the sorrows and agonies of life, spent a penance of seven years in the shade of the sacred Bodhi tree to attain enlightenment.

The Puning Temple is essentially Tibetan, an imitation of the Samye Monastery, and its main hall, the Mahayana Pavilion, is more than 118 ft. (36 m) high, surrounded by small pagodas and pavilions symbolizing the Four Corners and Eight Minor Corners of the universe, as interpreted by the Buddhist scriptures. In other halls to the southwest of the pavilion, the Qing emperors once rested and listened to Buddhist sermons. ◄

Xumi Fushou Temple

The Xumi Fushou Temple was built north of the Imperial Summer Villa in 1780 to accommodate the sixth Panchen lama when he traveled from Tibet for the seventieth birthday celebrations of the Qing emperor Qianlong. The temple is virtually a replica of the Trashilungpo Monastery in Kagaze, and its Chinese name is a translation meaning "with the longevity and well-being of Mount Xumi," a legendary mountain in Buddhist mythology. Occupying a total area of nearly 400,000 sq. ft. (37,000 sq. m), the temple's architecture is mainly Tibetan, with certain details modified into Han style. Calligraphy by emperor Qianlong, indicating the name of the temple, adorns the entrance. The main hall where the sixth Panchen Lama gave his sermons is located on the top of the three-tiered Big Red Terrace, while the lama's residence is located to the west. The temple also features, among other fanciful structures, a green-glazed Pagoda of Longevity, similar to the one in Fragrant Hill Park in Beijing. ▲

BASHANG
坝上

North of Beijing, all the way to the border of Inner Mongolia, the Bashang Plateau rises like a giant staircase at 4922 to 6890 ft. (1500 to 2100 m) above sea level. Bashang means "top of the dam" in Chinese, and the natural pastures of the Bashang Plateau are abundantly supplied with water and lush grass. One of the most scenic spots in the area is the Mulan Imperial Hunting Park north of Chengde City. This beautiful area, inhabited mostly by ethnic Mongolians, has been a retreat from the heat of Beijing summers in the past for emperors, imperial kinsmen and nobles who came to hunt and practice martial arts there. Now it is called the back garden of Beijing. For visitors, the pleasant weather and vast carpets of green grass are a welcome relief from the dust and heat in Beijing. The autumn colors of white bark birch, set against the deep green of pine and fir, are a delight not to be missed.

THE GREAT WALL

長城

Nothing can really compare to the immense human labor that went into the construction and almost constant renovation and expansion of the greatest of monument to Chinese civilization: the Great Wall.

Initiated during the Qin dynasty in the 3rd century BC, when the emperor ordered the linking up of older tribal walls, the Great Wall forced into labor some 500,000 peasants, among them many convicted criminals. In the later interim and unstable rule of the Northern Wei (AD 386-534), another 300,000 people were put to work on a single section south of Datong. In AD 607-608, when north-south political divisions were still shaking the foundations of Chinese unity, a full 1 million people were further called upon. But all this paled against the many millions of laborers conscripted during the Ming dynasty to modernize, strengthen and extend the wall—this stage of the project alone took more than 100 years to complete.

The result is nothing short of a human marvel, a man-made protective barrier that snakes a distance of 3728 mi. (6000 km) over and through the rumpled folds of the northern Chinese landscape from Shanhaiguan on the shores of the Bo Sea, through Hebei, Shanxi, Inner Mongolia, Shaanxi, Ningxia and Gansu provinces until it reaches Jiayuguan in the arid west. It is a monument to the human spirit and a memorial to immense human suffering. During each work campaign, thousands died of sickness, accident, exposure or simply the physical ordeal. Almost everything was done by hand, passing from one to another the raw materials—rock, earth, bricks, lime and timber—up mountainsides and along ridges to each worksite. Handcarts were used on flat land or gentle slopes, and goats and donkeys sometimes hauled the bricks and lime, but otherwise it was harsh and unremitting human toil that built this most spectacular man-made structure.

The Great Wall of the Warring Kingdoms

Long before the Great Wall itself was built, primitive defensive mounds and walls were thrown up here and there throughout northern China to protect tribal groups from surprise attack. According to ancient records, the state of Chu built walls in the 7th century BC in the areas that are now Henan and Hubei Provinces.

The Great Wall of the Warring Kingdoms emerged from several defensive lines of tamped earth built by the various states, and it was these unconnected walls that were joined together and strengthened to form the first stage of the Great Wall in the Qin dynasty. Pictured below is the Qi wall, built in the 5th century BC in what is now the province of Shandong. It runs from Pingyin in the west, around the northern slopes of Tai Mountain, and ends at the coast. ▼

Jiayuguan

The western reaches of the Great Wall terminate at a point to the southwest of Jiayuguan in the Gobi sands of Gansu Province. Jiayuguan or Jiayu Pass is located at the narrowest point of the western section of the Hexi Corridor. It is here that the Ming emperor Taizu built the Tianxia Xiongguan (the World's Greatest Fortress) in 1372 on the site of an earlier fortification that had been there since the time of the Han dynasty. It is said that the Ming engineers were so meticulous, and their specifications so exact, that when the new fort was completed, only a single brick remained. It has since been proudly displayed in one of the fort's halls.

This well-preserved stronghold and remote, desolate outpost on the edge of the wilderness is considered the gateway to the Chinese empire from the west. It consists of three defense lines—an inner city, an outer city and a moat. It covers an area of 360,600 sq. ft. (33,500 sq. m), with a wall 33 ft. (10 m) high surrounding it. There are two gates, on the eastern and western corners, each built into three-story gatehouses with single-eaved half-hipped roofs. Outside the west gate sits the stela that carries the four Chinese characters: Tian Xia Xiong Guan, while the east gate faces a few temples and a traditional theater stage.

As is true with most of the Great Wall's fortified points, Jiayuguan straddles a strategic pass between the Qilian and Heli mountain ranges. It was also an important access for the overland caravans of the Silk Route. ▲ ▶ ▶ ▶

Watchtowers of the Great Wall

There were two types of watchtowers built along the Great Wall—qiangtai (wall towers), which were erected on the wall itself or jutted from its sides, and ditai (enemy towers), which were two-story fortifications containing living quarters and arsenals and crenellated parapets. Many of these enemy towers can still be found along a 311 mi. (500 km) section of relatively intact wall in the northern part of Hebei Province. Designed by the Ming general Qi Jiguang, they were placed at short intervals, particularly between Juyongguan and Shanhaiguan. ▲

The Great Wall at Jinshan

One particularly well-defended stretch of the wall—now crumbling in many places—was built in 1570 by General Qi Jiguang to cover a series of low rolling hills at Jinshan. Because the open, gently rising terrain gave any enemy easy access to the Han hinterland, the wall along this 19-mi. (30-km) section was heavily strengthened and well fortified with watchtowers and beacon posts. ▶

Juyongguan

When the first emperor of Qin completed the first stage of the Great Wall's construction, he found he had another problem on his hands—many hundreds of unwanted laborers. He resettled them at Juyongguan in Changping County of what is now Hebei Province—the name Juyong believed to be a shortened version of Xi Ju Yong Tu, meaning "to resettle redundant people."

But Juyong has an important strategic place in history too. Flanked by high mountains and straddling a 12-mi.-long (20-km-long) gully, it was regarded as a vital linchpin in the defense of northern China and apparently so indomitable that it was the subject of at least one poetic tribute: "With only one soldier to defend the place, even ten thousand attackers will fail to capture it."

Near Juyong there is a terrace called Yuntai (Cloud Terrace) built in 1345 of white marble. It once supported three Buddhist stupas, which were destroyed around the time of the late Yuan (Mongol) dynasty. A nearby monastery, Taian, built in 1439, was burned down in 1702. What is left of Yuntai, the base, features an arched gate 23 ft. (7 m) high and wide enough for a carriage to be driven through. The facade is decorated with Buddhist images which were carved there during the Ming reign. ▼

Bada Range

The Bada Range (Eight-Reaching Pass) section of the Great Wall climbs high up a mountain range in the Yanqing area of Hebei and offers one of the best surviving examples of the Wall's defensive architecture and fortification. This area of the Wall and its garrison were built in 1505 in the reign of the Ming emperor, Xiaozong, and they were definitely built to last. The wall itself is higher than most other sections, rests on huge stone slabs and is constructed almost entirely of brick and stone. The parapets are crenellated, and the lower sections of the walls have loopholes for defensive fire by archers. The top surface of the wall is 16 ft. (5 m) wide, with space enough for five horses or 10 soldiers to march abreast along it. ▲

Shanhaiguan

Shanhaiguan is a strategic garrison built by the Ming general Xu Da in 1381 that lies at the far eastern end of the Great Wall, overlooking the Bo Sea. It is a powerful fortification, and rightly so, for it was regarded as the key to the capital itself. Aside from defensive walls, watchtowers and a central bell tower, the garrison features a two-story "arrow tower" for archers and some 68 loopholes along its south, east and north walls through which a constant hail of arrows could be directed at attacking forces. When not in use, these "arrow windows" were closed with red wooden shutters that had white disks and bull's eyes painted rather provocatively on them. With the Bo Sea to the south and the Great Wall snaking high into the adjacent mountains of the north— beginning its long march to the deserts of the west—

Shanhaiguan is one of the most dramatic points along the 3728 mi. (6000 km) fortification. As an old poem describes it:

I have heard of the great Shanhaiguan,
But only today are my eyes truly widened.
Ten thousand hectares of waves, one never
tires of watching
Countless peaks and ravines, they are
impossible to cross.

The picture on the right shows Lao Long Tou (Old Dragon Head), where the east end of the Great Wall reaches the ocean. ▲

The Western Region

The western region of China is an area of striking and somewhat bizarre physical contrasts. It is arid, yet rich in life-giving water resources. It covers vast areas of land that is flat, inhospitable and rated among the bleakest of the world's deserts—yet it also features massive snowcapped mountain ranges that roll like huge ocean waves into the Himalayas. It is an area of primary resources—minerals, salt, oil, chemicals and forest products—yet it is also the main setting for China's most advanced technology: its nuclear and aerospace centers. It has always been regarded as the main defensive frontier of Chinese civilization, yet it was once the Middle Kingdom's only channel of communication with Central Asia, the Middle East and the rest of the world.

It is an area of some 1.5 million sq. mi (4 million sq. km), embracing the Xinjiang Uygur Autonomous Region, Gansu, Qinghai and Tibet (Xizang). In the north it borders the (Outer) Mongolian People's Republic; to the west, Kazakhstan, and Jammu and Kashmir in northeast India; and to the south, Nepal, Bhutan and Burma. It features the highest river in the world, the Yalong, and one of the world's highest lakes, the Namu, which lies north of the Tibetan capital, Lhasa.

The Xinjiang Uygur Autonomous Region is divided by the Tian Mountains into two vast desert basins, the Tarim in the south and Junggar in the north. In the Tarim there lies one of the two most dreaded deserts in China, the Taklimakan, an 309,000-sq. mi. (800,000-sq. km) stretch of 328-ft. (100-m) high shifting dunes and fierce sandstorms. North of these basins lies the second most notorious desert waste, the Gobi, stretching northeast into Mongolia. In the southwest Xinjiang region, it is a waterless sea of dunes and so inhospitable that local people call it the "land of death." In central western Xinjiang, the desert surface plunges more than 494 ft. (150 m) below sea level to form the Turfan Depression, one of the lowest land surfaces on Earth.

Despite its hostile terrain, much of Xinjiang is also a vast underground freshwater cistern. Glaciers and melting snow from the region's four main mountain ranges, the Cong Range in the west, Altay in the northeast and Kunlun and Altun to the south, contribute to rivers that flow intermittently and frequently dry up and, more important, to immense underground reservoirs that feed surface springs, man-made wells and irrigation systems in surprisingly lush oases that dot the sands. These springs and wells have enabled no less than 13 minority groups in all, notably the Uygur, Kazakh, Huizu and tens of thousands of Han Chinese settlers to carve a solid foothold on the land.

The same water cycle saved many a trading caravan from perishing along another notorious stretch of the Silk Road. This mighty canyon, beginning in the Wushao Range in the east and carving its way through the land to Yumen Pass at the western extremity of the Great Wall, was one of central China's main thoroughfares to Central Asia and a natural entry point for armies of marauding Mongols. Because of its strategic importance, it came under imperial attention, with military and economic development from as early as the Han dynasty (206 BC–AD 220). The Great Wall itself is a prime military example.

Gansu also marks the point where the three tablelands of Mongolia, the loess (sandstone) area and Tibet converge. The great Yellow River rises in Tibet and cuts through the south of Gansu, creating the spectacular Liujia and Sangyuan Gorges. Along with the Yellow River, the mighty Yangtze, Lancang and Nu rivers of China begin there, and so do the sacred Ganges and Indus of India. The melting snows also feed more than 1500 lakes throughout the Ngari and Nanqu regions of northern Tibet, and in the high trans-Himalayan valleys of the south, it forms China's greatest lake, Qinghai Lake, in the northeastern corner of Qinghai Province.

Qinghai is well endowed with rivers, providing fine pastureland in the southeastern areas and rich agricultural land along the Hehuang Valley and wheatlands. Xining, the capital, is the gateway to the Qinghai-Tibet Plateau. From here the landscape mounts in huge peaked steps to the "roof of the world," lifting into five great mountain ranges—Kunlun, Karakorum, Tanggula, Gangdise and Nyainqentanglha—that culminate in the Himalayas.

Locked away in its Himalayan fortress, Tibet remains to be a mystery land with its unique highland scenery. It is culturally and ethnically a distinct region that has drawn people from all over the world. Highlights include Potala Palace and Dazao Monastery in Lhasa and the Drepung Monastery. Communication between the Tibetans and the Han Chinese goes back to the Tang dynasty (AD 618–907).

THE SNOW LOTUS
天山雪蓮

The Snow Lotus is one of very few plants that manage to flourish in a combination of thin air, bitter cold and increased ultraviolet light above the snow line of the Tian Mountain Range. An occasional burst of white petals with a slight yellow tint to them, it can be found in sheltered spots on slopes 9800 to 13,100 ft. (3000 to 4000 m) high. Its stem is smooth, and its roots are long, spreading deep into whatever earth it can find in the fissures and scars of the rocks in search of moisture and nourishment. Herbal pharmacists sell dried Snow Lotuses to mountain tribespeople, who soak them in spirits to prepare a concoction that they claim can cure backache, rheumatism and arthritis. ▷

THE TIAN MOUNTAIN RANGE
天山山脈

According to the Xiongnu people of the Xinjiang region—descendants of an ancient group of slave-owning nomad tribes—the Tian Range of mountains is "heaven." They also call them White Mountains or Snow Mountains and venerate them as their earth mother. Centuries ago, in the Han dynasty, the range was called the North Mountain, standing sentinel on the northwestern frontier of the infant Chinese nation-state against the marauding Xiongnu themselves.

The range rises in central Xinjiang and marches about 1550 mi. (2500 km) northwest into the heart of Kyrgyzstan and Kazakhstan. In Xinjiang it separates the Tarim and Junggar Basins, effectively dividing the autonomous region into northern and southern zones, and its lofty and precipitous path runs through other valleys and basins, such as the Turfan Depression, Hami, Yanqi and Ili. At its eastern perimeter there are strategic mountain passes, notably the Seven-Cornered Well Pass and Dabancheng Pass, which have served for centuries as vital Central Asian gateways to China.

Most of the Tian Range's peaks are 9800 to 16,400 ft. (3000 to 5000 m) high, with Mount Tomur (24,393 ft. or 7435 m) and Mount Hantengri (22,949 ft. or 6995 m) dominating the range in the west, and Mount Bogda (17,864 ft. or 5445 m) the highest in the east. The peaks are perennially snowbound, and there are an estimated 6896 glaciers in the range—an enormous reservoir of ice that, as it melts at the lower altitudes, becomes the fountainhead of rivers such as the Urumqi, Manas, Jing, Ili, Kaidu and Aksu. On the range's northern slopes are grasslands and several varieties of hardy high-altitude plants. Elsewhere, the slopes are rich in medicinal herbs, wildlife and minerals.

Sky Lake in the Tian Mountains

Not to be confused with Sky Lake in China's northeast, this smaller, oblong lake, only 1.9 mi. (3 km) long, lies on the slope of Mount Bogda, just under 6600 ft. (2000 m) above sea level. It was referred to in a Ming dynasty novel as the place where the Taoist Heavenly Queen Mother held her birthday party. It was named Sky Lake in 1783 when the governor of Xinjiang laid a stone monument inscribed with the words "heavenly mirror" and "godly pond."

Sky Lake was formed when debris from a glacier blocked a section of one of the rivers that carries melted snow from the upper slopes of Mount Bogda. The lake and its environs have become a popular holiday resort—a comfortable 59°F (15°C) in summer and a relatively warm ice-skating center in winter, even when the temperature on the northern slopes of the Tian Mountains plunges as low as −104°F (−40°C). The area around the lake is heavily wooded and contains a variety of valuable medicinal herbs. There are many scenic views and several Tibetan-style monasteries, notably Fushou Monastery, also called Iron-Tiled Monastery for its blue bricks and the gray metallic color of its tiles. ▲

HANAS LAKE
哈納斯

Much of the northwest of China remains a mystery. One of the jewels of the area is Hanas Lake, known only in the last 30 years to the outside world. It lies in the vast unspoiled forest on Altay Mountain (or gold mountain), in northern Xinjiang. Like many of the lakes and rivers in the region, it is formed from melted snow and is known as the most beautiful spot in the Uygur autonomous region, with a landscape said to match Switzerland. In fact, the word "hanas" in Mongolian means "beautiful, rich and mysterious." The mirror-flat mountain lake is famous for its changing color, dependent on vantage point, and the ever-changing weather, winning Hanas Lake the title "the lake of changing colors." Surrounding the lake, a 2100-sq. mi. (5500-sq. km) nature reserve is rich in animal and plant resources. The mystery of a legendary "lake monster" adds more to the attraction of this serene and secluded area, where one can enjoy all kinds of activities, from trekking, horseback riding, fishing, river valley drifting and camping. ▲

BAYANBULAK
巴音布鲁克

Nestled at the southern foothill of Tian Mountains, Bayanbulak, meaning "rich spring" in Mongolian, is a vast pastureland of 8880 sq. mi. (23,000 sq. km). The Mongolians live in this second largest grassland in China, together with eight other ethnic minority groups, raising special local breeds of animals suited to the high pasturelands, such as the Tian Shan horses, Bayanbulak sheep and yaks.

Rivers zigzag in these highland pastures 8200 ft. (2500 m) above sea level. In the heart of the highland basin lies the peaceful Swan Lake, in a vast marshland formed by many smaller lakes and ponds. It is now a national nature reserve, providing a safe haven for wild swans, some of them rare species, and more than 70 other year-round inhabitants and migrating birds. ▽ ▷

FLAMING MOUNTAINS (HUOYAN SHAN)
火焰山

A vivid example of the intense heat of the desolate Turfan Depression in Xinjiang is found in the Flaming Mountains in the north-central area of the basin, where the daytime temperature often reaches 158°F (70°C) and an egg can be fried on the scorching rock of the slopes. When the sun strikes the rock and red soil, the whole mountain range shimmers with the colors of fire, and deep vertical fissures in the slopes give the impression of tongues of flame licking the skies.

The mountains stretch east to west for about 62 mi. (100 km) across the Turfan Basin. ◄

Sugong Tower
蘇公塔

Dominating the southeastern skyline of the city of Turfan, this Buddhist monument, erected in 1778, is 131 ft. (40 m) high and constructed of yellow bricks in 15 different patterns, each forming a decorative band around the walls. It has no foundation stones and is supported instead by a central spiral brick pillar with steps leading up to a viewpoint at the top. Next to the tower is a building that is equally imposing—a monastery built to accommodate more than 1000 monks, students and worshippers. ▼

Lake Lop Nor
羅布泊

Over the past 2000 years the lower Tarim River in Xinjiang has changed its course three times, depending on the amount of snow-fed waters feeding into it. And as the river changed, so too did the position of Lake Lop Nor, the largest of China's saltwater lakes. The current location of this vast salt bed, surrounded by sand dunes and salt crusts, is on the eastern edge of the basin, bounded by the cities of Kuruktag, Yumen and Yangguan and Tikanlik.

But Lop Nor is really only a lake when the waters are available. Though its eastern extremity is submerged, forming many small lakes and marshes, it is generally regarded as simply a salt-covered lowland stretching over an area of about 1158 sq. mi. (3000 sq. km). It was an important landmark during the heyday of the Silk Road, and there are many historic temples, shrines and resting places on its shores. West of the lake is the site of an ancient trading center, Loulan. Fierce winds from the Central Asian steppes ravage the lake's northeastern extremities, whipping up huge dunes of salt and then carving them into spectacular pillars. ▲

RUINS OF JIAOHE
交河故城

The dust-dry climate of the Turfan Depression has helped preserve more than one important historical relic, and notable among them are the ruins of a Uygur tribal city at Jiaohe, west of Turfan County. Constructed in the Tang dynasty of mud-brick and rammed earth, enough of the main structure still stands today to give a clear picture of the thoroughfares and lanes, official halls, monasteries and pagodas, homes and courtyards, corridors and underground passages and thick earthen defensive walls of what was, in fact, a relatively sophisticated settlement. Underground chambers were dug below each dwelling to give shelter from the fierce daytime heat.

The ruins stand at the junction of two riverbeds and are overshadowed by a 98-ft. (30-m) high sheer cliff, the edge of a plateau, which was obviously an effective barrier against invasion. The town was abandoned in the latter part of the Yuan dynasty, perhaps as a result of Han military pressure on the northern remnants of the preceding Mongol rule. ▲

RUINS OF GAOCHANG
高昌故城

Gaochang, another mud-brick ruin to the east of Turfan County, was once the capital of the state of Ouigour and an important way station on the Silk Route. It stood as a strategic political, economic and cultural center of the western frontier until the Ming dynasty when, like the settlement at Jiaohe, it was abandoned. From what is left of it today, it is obvious that it played an important military role on the frontier—it is surrounded by two defensive walls, the outer one standing from 13 ft. (4 m) to 36 ft. (11 m) high and 39 ft. (12 m) thick in some places. The remains of a huge monastery can be seen at the southwest corner of the wall, close to the ruins of a tower that stood 49 ft. (15 m) high. ◄

THE BEZIKLIK GROTTOES
柏孜克里克石窟

The vitality with which Buddhism flowed through this Central Asian gateway to inner China can be appreciated in the dramatic Beziklik Grottoes, which lie on the slopes of a range of hills about 31 mi. (50 km) northeast of Turfan. They were probably built during the early flowering of the religion in China, in the time of the divided North and South dynasties of AD 420–589, before the rise of the powerful Tangs. Among the 64 grottoes that were either cut into the hillside or built of mud-brick and rammed earth, there are Buddha shrines and places of worship and cells that provided meditation retreats for the monks.

But the main feature of this sacred complex is the murals that adorn the walls of many of the chambers, most of which are in poor condition, but a great many have withstood the ravages of time. They depict standing Buddhas, Bodhisattvas in the state of Nirvana, musicians, Buddhist and local folklore and, in one particular grotto, a dilapidated painting that is believed to be the only cave mural in China dealing with Judgment and Hell. ▼

MULTI-COLORED BAY (WUCAIWAN)

五彩灣

Wucaiwan, or literally Five Color Bay, is known for the exotic colors of the surrounding mountains and unique shape of the terrain. This expanse of outcrops, which used to be an ancient lake in the Jurassic period, lies deep in the heart of the Gurbantunggut Desert east of the Junggar Basin. A geological phenomenon formed by wind and water erosion, Wucaiwan draws evocative names identifying the great variety of outcrops, such as Multi-colored City, Petrified Trees and Huoshao Shan, which means "fire-burned mountain."

Multi-colored City, or Wucaicheng, is the core of this rustic badland, covering an area of a little over 1 sq. mi. or 3 sq. km. The rolling range of hills and knolls from 33 to 131 ft. (10 to 40 m) high are extremely colorful. They look like pyramids, fortresses, palaces, and pavilions, hence the name of the place. Huoshao Shan, on the other hand, is a small range of red mountains said to be covered millions of years ago with a layer of coal, which was set on fire by the heat of the blazing sun. When the fire burned completely, what was left were exposed red rocks and hills that appear to glow in the early morning or late afternoon light, as if still burning.

Apart from colorful rock formations, large quantities of fossilized dinosaurs have been found in Wucaiwan, together with petrified trees. Some trees are still laden with fruits that are now petrified.

Some areas in Wucaiwan are still off the beaten track, but hardy visitors who dare to venture out into the wilderness will be more than compensated by the famous bright colors here. ▲

UYGUR TOMB
阿帕克和卓墓

The strong Islamic influence throughout China's western region—an influence going back to the Mongol Yuan dynasty's links with the Moslem empire—can be seen in the stunning architecture of the 17th century Uygur Tomb on the outskirts of Kashi. It began as a family mausoleum, and today it presents a striking contrast of rustic simplicity and the ornate architecture of Islam—the eastern colors of its cone-shaped graves adding splendor to the principal grave chamber, a beautiful domed tomb decorated with green and amber tiles with minaret-style towers on all four corners. This main tomb contains 72 graves, most of them decorated with mosaic tiles and draped with colorfully patterned shrouds. One of them, as legend has it, contains the costumes of Xiangfei (Fragrant Concubine), a famous beauty who was kidnapped and installed in the Qing imperial court. ◄ ▼

THE WINE FOUNTAIN (JIUQUAN)
酒泉

Like the Great Wall of China, the Wine Fountain, situated in a park of the same name in the Hexi Corridor of Gansu Province, reflects the abiding fear of invasion from the north. Throughout the Han dynasty, a confederation of slave-owning nomad tribes called the Xiongnu constantly harassed the frontier. It is recorded that when the Han general Huo Qubing defeated the Xiongnu in a punitive war, Emperor Wu commanded that a large cask of wine be awarded to him for celebration. General Huo, wishing to share the wine with his soldiers, poured it into a spring, and they all drank it from there. According to inscriptions on a stela that now stands nearby, the local villagers also found that the waters tasted like wine, and so gave the spring its name.

The Wine Fountain is fed by underground waters that flow by way of the Beida and Hongshui rivers from the snows of Qilian Mountain. Its waters are crystal clear and do not freeze over in winter, a vital life-saving attribute, being one of the harshest sections of the Silk Route. A lake lies not far from the spring, fringed with white willows and tamarisks and beautified with a small bridge, an ornamental "zigzag" pathway and three pavilions. ▼ ▶

WEN TEMPLE OF WUWEI
武威文廟

The Wen Temple complex in Wuwei County, Gansu was built in 1437 and has since been renovated several times. The complex is 558 ft. (170 m) long and 295 ft. (90 m) wide, occupying an area of 183,000 sq. yd. (153,000 sq. m). One of the last major rebuilding projects took place during the reign of the Qing emperor Shunzhi.

There are two symmetrically arranged sections to the temple: two shrine halls on the east and Dacheng Hall, pictured above, on the west. Standing on a high brick-and-concrete platform, the hall features a double-eaved, half-hipped and half-gabled roof supported by cantilever brackets. A stela now erected in the temple is the largest and the best-preserved stela with inscriptions in ancient Xixia script. It is 9 ft. (2.6 m) high, 3.3 ft. (1 m) wide and 12 in. (30 cm) thick. On the front, in Xixia script inscribed in the year 1094, is a detailed account of the reconstruction of a pagoda that was ruined by an earthquake; on the back is a translation in the Han language. ▲

QINGHAI LAKE
青海湖

With no less than 50 rivers and streams flowing into Qinghai Lake, it is not surprising that it is rated the largest inland body of water in China. Its surface covers an area of 1776 sq. mi. (4600 sq. km), and it lies 10,500 ft. (3200 m) above sea level. Around its shores are vast marshes and grasslands that the local inhabitants, mainly Tibetans, regard as especially fine pasture for sheep and cattle. A Tibetan community inhabits one of the five islands in the lake, Haixin Hill, a granite outcrop that rises 250 ft. (76 m) above the water. It is a sacred spot and includes a temple. Another island, Bird Island (Niaodao), in the western reaches of the lake, is a haven for migratory birds such as spotted wild ducks. Thousands of them flock to the island and the food-rich marshes around the lake in March and April, to be joined by huge flocks of "fish gulls," brown-headed gulls, cormorants and swans. ▲ ▶

WHITE HORSE MONASTERY, QINGHAI
青海白馬寺

The horse is said to have originated in either Africa or Central Asia. But whatever its birthplace, its Asian contemporary, the Mongolian pony, has been valued and revered for centuries by the Chinese and their nomadic northern neighbors for its strength and endurance and military qualities. It is also one of the Seven Treasures of Chinese Buddhism and is paid due respect by the Buddhists of Tibet and Qinghai Province at the White Horse Monastery, built into the lower slope of a towering cliff to the east of Qinghai's capital, Xining.

The horse is also included in the pharmacopoeia of Chinese medicine, with the pure white breeds said to have the most powerful medicinal qualities. In the *Ben Cao*, or *Chinese Materia Medica*, published in 1596, it says: "The heart, when dried and powdered and taken with wine, is a certain cure for forgetfulness.... Above the knees the horse has night-eyes (warts) which enable him to travel in the night; they are useful in the toothache. If a man be hysterical when he wishes to sleep, let the ashes of a skull be mingled with water and given him, and let him have a skull for a pillow and it will cure him." ▼

TAER MONASTERY
塔爾寺

The Taer Monastery on the slope of Lotus Blossom Hill (Lianhua) in Huangzhong County is one of the largest lamaseries in Qinghai. It is also one of the most splendid examples of Tibetan Buddhist architecture and decor in the whole of the north and northwest. It was built in 1560 in memory of the founder of the Yellow Sect of lamaism, Tsongkhapa, and has been renovated and expanded several times since. It now comes under the Tibetan Gong Bem classification, meaning "a hundred-thousand Buddha images" for the many carved brick Buddha images of the chorten, or stupa, that dominates the center of the complex.

As with most lamaseries in China, there are latter-day Han as well as traditional Tibetan influences in the design. The main shrine hall is a Han-style structure with a triple-eaved, half-hipped and half-gabled roof, with walls decorated in bright green glazed tiles. In 1711 the roof was retiled in gilded copper, thanks to a donation by a Mongol prince. A silver chorten dedicated to Tsongkhapa stands in the center of the hall draped with yellow banners. The ceiling is a large mural of Buddhist scriptural tales, and the four walls are lined with several hundred volumes of the sutras.

The Taer monastery is also known for excellence in butter sculptures. This unique art form goes back thousands of years and usually features religious figures, animals, and flowers. Elegance and great details are the trademark attributes of these works (top, opposite). A butter sculpture festival is held annually here. Another special festival held twice a year here is the Bathing Buddha Festival, during which a giant portrait of Buddha is unfurled on a hillside facing the monastery (below). ▲

Great Sutra Hall (Dajingtang)

The Great Sutra Hall is the Taer Monastery's principal building, a typical flat-roofed Tibetan structure erected in 1606. It was destroyed by fire in 1913 and rebuilt four years later with a total of 168 columns, some of them set into the walls, decorated with ornate carvings or hung with colored rugs and embroidered pennants and streamers. The hall features a main theater with prayer mattresses for 2000 lamas. The walls are packed with volumes of the sutras and more than 1000 gilded copper Buddha images. All in all, the Taer Monastery includes the Great Gold Tile Monastery, Little Gold Tile Monastery, Little Flower Monastery, Great Sutra Hall, shrine halls and a series of kitchens and dormitories. ▼

QILIAN MOUNTAINS
祁連山

The Qilian Mountain Range extends over 620 mi. (1000 km) between Qinghai and Gansu provinces, a series of parallel mountain walls that include the Tulai, Lenglong Range, Datong, and South Tulai mountains. The highest peak, soaring to 19,000 ft. (5800 m), is in the South Tulai Range, and the average height of the others is about 14,760 ft. (4500 m). The whole range is snow-capped, includes more than 3300 glaciers and is the main source of water for the areas west of the Yellow River. The wide valleys are crisscrossed with streams, and there are many lakes, the largest being Qinghai and Har.

At their lower levels the Qilian Mountains are heavily forested with firs and cedars, and the gentler slopes provide good pasture for sheep, cattle and horses. The mountains were once a stronghold of the Xiongnu alliance of tribes. When they were conquered and pushed out of the hills by the Han general Huo Qubing, a poem lamented their defeat.

"Having lost our Qilian Mountain, we have nowhere to breed our animals. Deprived of our Yanzhi* Mountain, our women are losing their true colors." ▲

*Yanzhi can also mean "rouge."

WHITE PAGODA HILL (BAITA SHAN)
白塔山

Rising to the north of Lanzhou City in Gansu, this hill is named after the White Pagoda on its peak—a 500-year-old structure that centuries of violent earthquakes have failed to destroy. The pagoda was built during the reign of the Ming emperor Jingzong (1450–1456) and stands within a terraced Buddhist complex that includes three shrine halls and two monasteries. Its position commands a view of the Yellow River and the entire city of Lanzhou. The hill itself rises from the north bank of the river to an altitude of 5580 ft. (1700 m). On the slope below the pagoda lie two strategic garrison gates, Jincheng (Golden City) and Yudie (Jade Heap). ◀

JINGANG HALL
五泉山金剛殿

On his way to the war against the Xiongnu, General Huo Qubing is said to have bivouacked his troops at what is now known as Five Springs Hill in the southern district of Lanzhou in Gansu Province. His troops were thirsty, and there was no water to be found. The general, according to the story, pulled his sword and struck a rock. Water gushed from it, and thus Five Springs Hill entered the vast realm of Chinese folklore.

Since then the hill and its springs have become an important Buddhist center. The Chongqing, Mani and Kitigarbha monasteries now stand there alongside the Sanjiao and Thousand Buddha Caves and various terraces and pavilions. Many of the original buildings were destroyed by border warfare against the Xiongnu "Huns," but the complex was restored in the reign of the Qing emperor Tongzhi in the years after 1868. The Jingang shrine hall is the oldest structure, erected in 1372 in the reign of Emperor Taizu of the Ming dynasty, and is the principal hall of the Chongqing Monastery. ▲

MAIJI MOUNTAIN
麥積山

Lying southeast of Tianshui County in Gansu, Maiji is one of the hills at the western edge of the Qin Range. It is also the site of an inestimable wealth of buried treasures. In the years AD 384–417, hundreds of Buddhist grottoes were cut into the side of the hill. In AD 734, during the reign of Tang emperor Xuanzong, part of the cliff-face collapsed in a violent earthquake, burying many of the caves and the images, murals and other Buddhist artwork within them.

In 1941 a team of Chinese historians made the first serious study of the Maiji grottoes, and in 1952 a party of archeologists, accompanied by artists and photographers, carried out another survey to see if the sealed sections could be excavated. They found, however, that the cliff face was too precipitous and dangerous—the cliff leans outward about 26 ft. (8 m) at its peak—and so the treasures inside have remained buried.

In the 194 grottoes that survived the earthquake, more than 7000 clay and stone sculptures and 1555 sq. yd (1300 sq. m) of murals have been found. The largest clay images are more than 49 ft. (15 m) tall. Of the murals, one of the most elaborate and interesting is that of a horse pulling a carriage, which appears to change the direction of its walk as the viewer changes position. ▲

YAMZHO YUMCO

羊卓雍錯

Yamzho Yumco, in the Lhoka area of Tibet, is one of Tibet's three holy lakes. Yamzho Yumco means Green Jade from the Upper Pasture, but it is also called Swan Lake after the swans that make the lake their home. Yamzho Yumco is the smallest of the three holy lakes, the other two being Nam Co (Heavenly Lake) and Mapam Yumco (Unsurpassed Lake). Ringed by majestic snow-capped peaks, visitors to Yamzho Yumco are thrilled to find tranquil islands, rare birds, many wild animals, rare plants, hot springs and ancient monasteries. The lake lies at 14,570 ft. (4441 m) above sea level, and its 246 sq. mi. (638 sq. km) seen from above resemble a giant piece of jade nestled in the northern slopes of the Himalayas.

All three holy lakes have inspired fairy tales; Yamzho Yumco's features a fairy maiden turned into a swan for violating celestial laws. Other goddesses comforted her by coming to bathe in the lake. Nam Co is named for Nyaintanglha, the consort of the guardian of the native Bon religion of Tibet, while Mapam Yumco, also called Emerald Pond, is where the Chinese Heavenly Mother of the West resides, according to ancient Tibetan writing.

TRASHILUNGPO MONASTERY

札什倫布寺

One of the most interesting and historic Buddhist institutions in Tibet, the Trashilungpo Monastery, was erected by Gedun Truppa, the first Dalai lama. It serves also as the tomb of the fourth Panchen lama and has been a religious and political center since his death. Among its most treasured relics are volumes of the Buddhist canon of scriptures written on palm leaves and elaborate silk tapestries of the Yuan and Ming dynasties. Situated southwest of Xingaze, close to Tibet's southern border with Bhutan, the monastery covers an area of 23,921 sq. yd. (20,000 sq. m) and comprises a palatial assembly hall and a scriptural hall, or theological college, along with numerous shrine halls—one of which houses a 85-ft. (26-m) high bronze image of the Champa Buddha. ▼

DREPUNG MONASTERY

哲蚌寺

Drepung in Tibetan means "large heap of rice"—not a very flattering comparison but one that manages to capture the white exterior decor and general design of this, one of the three greatest lamaseries of the Gelu, or Yellow Sect of Tibetan Buddhism. The monastery stands on a mountain slope about 3 mi. (5 km) west of the Tibetan capital, Lhasa. It was built in 1416 by command of the sect's founder, Tsongkhapa. The principal architecture is Tibetan and traditionally flat-roofed, but the main buildings incorporate Chinese-style gilded Buddhist wheels and other ornamentation.

The Drepung monastery is huge, accommodating 7700 lamas, and it includes different departments for education, ceremony and academic and general affairs. Its sutra hall alone is so enormous that between 8000 and 9000 lamas can pray and chant there at a time. ▲

POTALA PALACE
布達拉宮

This massive fortified palace and monastery, the "Vatican" of Tibetan Buddhism, looms across the crest of the Red Hill to the northeast of Lhasa. Construction began in the 7th century when the Prince of Tubo, Songsten Gampo, built what was then known as the Red Roofed Palace in honor of his Chinese consort, Princess Wencheng.

In 1642 the fifth Dalai Lama rebuilt the entire complex—pressing 7000 slaves into what turned out to be a full 50 years of work—as the seat of Tibetan Buddhism and government. Since then, Potala has comprised two main sections, known as the Red and White Palaces, with the White Palace housing the Dalai Lamas and their vast courts of priests and monks and the Red Palace containing shrines, libraries and halls of worship. The buildings at the foot of the hill include administrative offices, workshops, a printing press and a prison.

As a palace-castle complex, Potala is as security-conscious as it is sacred. Walls of enormous granite blocks protect it, along with a number of fortresses. As an added precaution, the walls are said to be reinforced with copper to strengthen them against earthquakes. ▲

The Sun Hall of the Potala

Despite its altitude and the bitter cold of winter, Lhasa is known as the Sun City of Tibet for the long hours of daylight that it enjoys, about twice that of any other place in the same latitude. For this reason the living quarters of the Dalai Lama were built in the White Palace on the top of the Potala. It is named the Sun Hall because the hall enjoys abundant sunlight through its spacious windows. It's here, in comfortable and ornate surroundings, that the supreme rulers spent their winter months.

These living quarters have been well preserved and extensively renovated. Every year thousands of visitors, most of them from the West, have filed through the Potala and the Sun Hall since Tibet was reopened to foreigners in 1980, to view the magnificent apartment and such decor and relics as the wands, lined with tiger fur, that are the Dalai Lamas' symbol of absolute authority; the predominant red and gold decoration of the rooms and their many priceless tapestries, carpets, murals and sculptures of Buddhas and Bodhisattvas; the intricate carvings of the screens and furnishings and the vivid splashes of color from the woven and embroidered pillar rugs.

All the gold and silver utensils used by successive Dalai Lamas are on display, along with teacups and bowls of carved jade, amber bowls and gold and silver goblets, and gold vases that weigh up to 8.8 lb. (4 kg) apiece. The throne of the Dalai Lama stands on the north side of the hall, and beside it are placed a human-skin drum and a wine bowl made from a human skull—tokens of his power and influence. Though certainly bizarre to Westerners, the use of human bones in this fashion is, in fact, a venerated tradition of Tibetan Buddhism. In traditional death ceremonies, for example, corpses are left exposed on mountain slopes to be picked clean by animals and birds. The bones are then smashed and flung into ravines, symbolizing the conviction that it is the spirit, traveling toward reincarnation, that is sacred; the worldly remains are of no importance at all. ▼

Norbu Lingka
羅布林卡湖心宮

Norbu Lingka itself is a white-walled villa complex, which in Tibetan is called "Treasure Garden". It lies less than a mile west of Potala Palace. The industrious 7th Dalai Lama, obviously following the tradition set by the Chinese emperors, built this seasonal retreat on what until then had been a grove of brambles. He designed it in three sections, the palace, monasteries and a well-laid park of ponds, pavilions and scenic pathways. His successor added a Mid-Lake Palace, built in the Chinese architectural style—a series of ornate buildings and pavilions resting on a podium 6 ft. (2 m) above the waters of the lake. With its traditional Chinese décor of dark jade-colored tiles and red columns, the palace stands out most effectively against its wooded backdrop. ▶

Dazao (Jokhank) Monastery

大昭寺

There are many stories about the origin of Dazao Monastery in Lhasa. One recounts why it was built on what was once a lake. Long ago, King Songsten Gampo stood by a lake and made a promise to build a Buddhist temple for his first wife, the Nepalese Princess Bhrikuti. He took a ring, tossed it and vowed to build the monastery wherever the ring stopped rolling. The ring did not stop rolling on the shore of the lake; it rolled right into the water! Thousands of goats carried countless loads of earth to the lake to fill it in for the foundation of Dazao Monastery.

In another story the Chinese princess, Wencheng, bride of King Songsten Gampo, came to Tibet with a large wedding dowry. Part of the dowry was a statue of Sakyamuni (the historical Buddha) as a child. This story explains why the monastery was once named Jokhank Monastery, meaning "Buddhist temple," which was later built around the statue of the Buddha as a child. Tibetans believe that the Buddha himself made the statue.

Whichever story is true, Dazao Monastery is definitely one of the oldest wood-and-earth structures in Tibet, housing some of the rarest cultural and musical relics of Tibet dating back to the 7th century. While it is not as grand as the Potala Palace, it is the most important Buddhist temple in Lhasa. The Great Prayer Festival (smon-lam) is held here annually. During the festival the temple overflows with worshippers. ◄ ▲

SELA MONASTERY
色拉寺

Along with the Drepung and Gandan Monasteries, the Sela Lamasery in the northern district of Lhasa is one of the Three Great Monasteries of Tibetan Buddhism. It is also one of the six Gelu, or Yellow Sect lamaseries—its lamas wearing yellow caps to signify membership of this particular Buddhist following. The name Sela comes from the origins of the monastery: According to records, the site on which it stands was a big orchard abundant with a citrus fruit called *se*. It is said that when Tsongkhapa, the father of the Yellow Sect, was riding through the grove, his horse neighed three times—and he interpreted this as meaning that in three years' time the Horse Headed Heavenly Guard, a guardian spirit of Buddhism and a reincarnation of Avalokitesvara Buddha, would descend to earth. Tsongkhapa ordered that a shrine hall be erected on the spot.

Later, one of his disciples, Jamchen Choje, built the Sela Monastery itself, with the Horse-Headed god as its main deity. Other interesting Buddhist relics and treasures in the lamasery include a silver chorten containing the remains of a Dalai Lama and, decorated with jewelry and precious stones, a Tibetan sutra written in gold and a set of sandalwood figures of the Buddhist deities brought from Beijing by the monastery's founder, Jamchen Choje.

The shrine hall (opposite, top) was the principal assembly hall of the monastery. Its dominant role and position in the arrangement of buildings distinguishes it from the others. ▲

MOUNT QOMOLANGMA
珠穆朗瑪峰

Himalaya Range is the highest mountain range on earth and yet one of the youngest. It boasts 1471 peaks, 229 of which are more than 22,960 ft. (7000 m) above sea level. Mount Qomolangma, the mightiest mountain in the world at 29,029 ft. (8848 m), is called Everest by Westerners who see it as a supreme test of courage and endurance and is regarded as the Goddess of the Snow Mountains by Tibetans, who venerate it for its beauty and grandeur. Over the centuries they have built palaces and gardens around its lower slopes—and a lamasery called Rongbu, which has the distinction of being the loftiest religious institution in the world.

Everest, or Qomolangma, is often shrouded by clouds and mist, which the Tibetans say is the "veil of the Holy Mother." For Western expeditions, these swirling mists are one of Everest's terrors, along with hurricane-force winds and storms that suddenly lash the snow and ice-covered slopes, the bitter temperatures (normally between 86°F or 66°C and 104°F or 76°C below zero), the lack of oxygen on the upper precipices and the summit itself, which is little more than a precarious ridge about 3ft. (1 m) wide and 39 ft. (12 m) long—a tiny pinhead at the very roof of the world.

On the Tibetan side of Mount Qomolangma, there are 217 glaciers and one vast stretch of the slopes, between 18,701 ft. (5700 m) and 21,982 ft. (6700 m), which is literally a forest of ice. Its "trees" are huge columns and towers of frozen runoff. Beyond this, at 24,606 ft. (7500 m), it is so cold and bleak that much of Everest's face is simply craggy and precipitous bare rock. ▲ ▶

THE SILK ROAD

絲路

Chinese silk has been admired the world over since time immemorial, yet each bale of the precious material that ever reached the West in times past had to make a perilous journey across thousands of miles of desert wastes and Central Asian steppes along that most romantic of all trade routes, the Silk Road (or Silk Route).

A major expansion of China's silk trade with the West came about as a result of military endeavor. The Han dynasty emperor Wu, who reigned from 140–88 BC, sent envoys into what is now Uzbekistan in search of fabled "blood-sweating" horses, said to have descended from the heavens, to aid him in his wars against Xiongnu and Mongol incursions on the northern and western frontiers. His decision turned out to be a wise one, for in one campaign after another these sturdy fleet-footed Mongol ponies pushed back the Huns until they were finally expelled from the entire Gansu region. This military success opened up the route that the first western-bound trading caravans took, setting out in 114 BC and soon followed by many others until 12 trading expeditions were pushing west through the deserts each year. Each caravan consisted of roughly a hundred merchants, emissaries and retainers, along with a train of camels each capable of car-

rying loads of up to 300 lb. (140 kg) for up to 19 mi. (30 km) a day.

The name Silk Road was coined by the German scholar Ferdinand Von Richthofen. The trade route, or routes since there were many routes that headed in an east-west direction, began in Xi'an and passed along the Hexi corridor to the oasis at Dunhuang and then on to Yumenguan (Jade Gate) at the westernmost point of the Great Wall. From there it divided into two routes, giving caravans a choice of going north or south of the dreaded Taklimakan Desert. The northern trail struck out across the desert toward Hami. Hugging the foothills of the Tian Mountain Range, it passed through Turpan, Karashahr, Kucha, Aksu and Tumchuq to Kashi. The southern trail followed the fringes of the Tibetan plateau, traveling via the oases at Miran, Endere (Tuhoho), Niya (Minfeng), Keriya (Yutian), Khotan (Hotian) and Yarkant (So Che). From there it turned northward to rejoin the northern route at Kashi.

From here the Silk Road continued westward and climbed the dangerous High Pamirs before passing out of Chinese territory into what is now Central Asia, continuing via Khokang, Samarkand, Bokhara and Merv through Persia and Iraq and on to the Mediterranean coast.

Xi'an's City Wall

The modern city of Xi'an, which lies to the southeast of Shaanxi Province, was known as Changan and served as the ancient Chinese capital from the time of the 11th century BC rule of the Western Chou to the triumph of the Tangs. From the 3rd century BC, it was also a vital commercial center because of its position on the eastern stretches of the Silk Route. Its trading importance and its vulnerability—lying in the path of the main Central Asian conduit into the heart of central China—also made it one of the most heavily fortified cities of the north.

From its earliest days, a defensive wall encircled it, and in 1374 when the large program of defensive works was undertaken by the Ming, the city's present wall was built—a massive stone structure, strengthened with fortifications, running for about 7 mi. (12 km) around Xi'an, rising 40 ft. (12 m) high and spreading 45 to 60 ft. (14 to 18 m) thick at its base. They include some 98 watchtowers and nearly 6000 crenels cut into a parapet that runs right around the top of the wall. There are four huge gates, over which the Ming dynasty engineers built small multistory forts with observation points and firing ports, from which teams of archers and other defenders could shower the attacking forces with arrows, gunpowder bombs and blazing oil and naphtha. ◄

Mingsha Hills

Four mi. (6 km) south of Dunhuang and close to the Crescent Moon oasis, the fierce winds of the desert have whipped the sands into a series of tall and dramatically shaped dunes called Mingsha Hills. Legend has also added to the drama of this strangely beautiful place. The name of the dunes translates as "murmuring sand", referring to a noise like distant thunder that comes from the action of the wind on the sail-like curves that it has sculptured in the dunes' faces. It is said that there was once a general who set up camp here on his way to the Western frontier. During the night, a violent sandstorm blew up and buried him along with his army. The "murmur" from the dunes is said to be the cries of the buried souls. ▲

Dafangpancheng

Windswept sun-baked ruins of mud-brick walls are all that are left of Dafangpancheng, a garrison built in the Han dynasty roughly 2000 years ago between Dunhuang and Yumenguan in the Gobi Desert. The stronghold had considerable strategic value, standing close to the western terminal of the Great Wall and providing storage for provisions, equipment and fodder for the Han defenders based at other garrisons and watchtowers in the Yumenguan area. It also served as a way station on the Silk Route. When traders began using another trail that ran across the northern area of Gansu Province, Dafangpancheng and other towns around it fell into decline. ▷

Jade Gate (Yumenguan)

In the Han era, Yumenguan was a gateway to Central Asia and the principal market for jade from all over Xinjiang. But when the trade shifted away to the north, the city fell into ruin, and since the Tang dynasty, there has been much argument about where it actually stood. It was only recently, with the discovery of important Han dynasty documents in Dunhuang, that scholars were able to agree that ancient Jade Gate—not to be confused with modern Yumen Town and Yumen City—was located on what is now the site of Little Fangpancheng.

Yumenguan represented the boundary between civilized Han China and the dangerous barbarian lands of the Western frontier. The autobiography of Ban Chao in the latter part of the Han dynasty speaks of the area as if it were the very edge of the world. "Your Majesty's subject," he wrote, "does not hope to come to the Wine Springs, but does wish to cross the Yumenguan while still alive." ▲

Ancient Altar (Gujitai)

Six mi. (10 km) west of Turfan, a monolith of mud-brick and rammed earth rears up out of the boundless desolation, standing in tribute to the glory of the Silk Road, the Buddhist faith that took root along it, and those who survived the grueling journeys to and from the West. This massive altar forms the centerpiece of the ruins of Jiaohe, a strategic Silk Road city during the Han and Tang dynasties. Jiaohe and Gaochang were among dozens of cities and towns that sprang up along this section of the trade route, their populations ranging from a few hundred to as many as 10,000. When the busy overland route eventually succumbed to competition from the seas—a death knell that sounded during the great ocean-trading expeditions of the Ming dynasty—these centers became ghost towns and were gradually engulfed by the desert sands. Around the Ancient Altar, the ruins of Jiaohe have weathered the centuries reasonably well, and it is still possible to trace the sites of public buildings, streets and defensive walls. ▶

The Mogao Grottoes

Some of the greatest of China's Buddhist art treasures are found in the Mogao Grottoes, or Thousand Buddha Caves, cut into the precipitous eastern slope of Mingsha Mountain about 15 mi. (25 km) southeast of Dunhuang. The earliest grotto was built in AD 366 by the monk Lochuan, and more than a thousand others were added in the following centuries. By the year AD 698 the complex was already so well established that Li Huairang produced an account called "Renovating the Buddhist Shrines in Mogao Grottoes."

Today only 492 grottoes remain, but they are packed with treasures—murals covering a total area of 53,820 sq. yd. (45,000 sq. m), 3400 bas relief and three-dimensional wall sculptures, several thousand pillars with the lotus motif, and floral floor tiles and five ornate wooden shrines built in the Tang dynasty. In 1900 a Taoist priest named Wang Yuanlo opened up a sealed grotto and found some 50,000 Buddhist relics dating from the Jin to Song dynasties—scriptural texts, portraits, books, embroideries and much more.

The sculptural figures in the various caves are made of clay and painted, and they range in height from a few inches (centimeters) to 108 ft. (33 m). The murals present a wide and colorful range of subjects, including gloomy and mysterious stories from the 5th to 7th centuries, exuberant and more refined paintings of the Buddhist scriptures from the period after the Sui dynasty (AD 581–618) and two particular murals showing an ancient map of Wutai Mountain and the "journey of Zhan Yichao and his wife." ▶

Crescent Moon Spring (Yueyaquan)

This desert oasis lies among towering sand dunes about 4 mi. (7 km) south of Dunhuang and is said to be the place where the Emperor Wu of the Han dynasty found the coveted "blood-sweating" Wusun horses with which he was able to defeat and subdue the tribes of the Western frontier. It is a small spring, only 328 ft. (100 m) long and 82 ft. (25 m) wide, but is fed so abundantly with subterranean water that it has never been known to dry up, even in the fiercest sandstorms. As the *Dunhuang County Gazette* describes it: "It is beautiful and unfathomably deep (and) remains clear, though threatened sometimes by tumultuous conditions of the surrounding dunes."

Rushes grow around the water's edge, and there are trees on the east bank. In the spring the small lake becomes a popular visiting spot, especially at the time of the Duanwu (also called Dragon Boat) Festival when pilgrimages are made to the nearby Mingsha Hill. The crescent-shaped spring is also noted for one of its inhabitants, the "iron-back" fish, and an herb called "seven star," both of which have health-giving properties and have thus provided the lake with the name Medicinal Spring. ◀

Polychrome Sculpture of Dunhuang

Clay was used for the wall sculptures of the Mogao Grottoes, either in Yingsu, or bas-relief, or the three-dimensional Yuansu technique in which the work is detached completely from the wall. They represent different artistic styles from three separate historical periods.

Those sculptures from the first period, dating from the Northern Wei (AD 386-534), largely depict musicians attending to the Buddha, with characteristics that include straight high noses, long brows, large eyes, broad shoulders and flat chests and loose or diaphanous garments. The Bodhisattvas of this period are all male.

In the middle period, dating from the Sui to Tang dynasties, the Sui sculptures feature large heads, robust physiques and disproportionately short legs, while those of the Tang era reflect the high standards of beauty and embellishment of the art of that time.

The last period, or school of Buddhist art, found among the Mogao treasures is that of the period of the Five Dynasties (AD 907–960) right through to the final imperial reign of the Qings. ▼ ▶

Murals at Mogao Grottoes

Apart from the exquisite sculptures and frescoes in the 492 grottoes, almost every grotto contains a group of colorful paintings of Buddha, Bodhisattvas and other religious deities. The murals also depict traditional Chinese mythology and everyday life in medieval China, with paintings of dancers, hunting scenes, details of a legend, mountains and, sometimes, a portrait of the donor of the art. Very little is known of the artists who created the murals over this thousand-year period, although speculations point to local artists, artists who came to this area with exiled masters, specially commissioned central China artists or artists from the Five Dynasty art academy. ▼

The Kizi Kuqa Beacon Tower

Standing 6 mi. (10 km) west of Kuqa County, this ancient watchtower—or the weather-beaten remains of it—was one of many built along the southern arm of the Silk Road to protect traveling merchants and emissaries from bandits. It also stood sentinel against the Xiongnu tribes, which constantly probed and attacked the northern frontiers during the Han dynasty. The tower, constructed of rammed earth reinforced with timber and reeds, was linked to a regional office and a series of garrisons at Kuqa. In an emergency, observers put up flag and smoke signals to alert the forts. According to records found at Juyan and Dunhuang, six combinations of signals were used, involving flags, smoke and fire and drums. At the top of the ruin, wooden rafters can be seen jutting from the walls, suggesting that it once had a reconnaissance balcony. ▲

Bostan Lake

The ancient south Tianshan route of the Silk Road stretches along the northeast to the west border of the lake, com-manding a strategic position of the trade route. Bostan in Mongolian means "nomads like to stop here," and after a grueling, dangerous and very thirsty struggle through the southern reaches of the Gobi Desert, Bostan was undoubtedly paradise itself.

Lying in the Yanqi Basin south of the Tian Mountain Range, the lake is 34 mi. (55 km) long and 15 mi. (25 km) wide. With a 26,153-billion-gallon (9.9-billion-m³) capacity, it is the largest freshwater lake in Xinjiang. It lies in a high-level area, at an altitude of just over 3280 ft. (1000 m), and is frozen over in winter. The lake takes its waters from three rivers that cut through the parched terrain and are fed in turn from the snows of the Tian Mountains.

Bostan Lake provides oases and irrigation along its banks for the cultivation of melons, apricots, plums, peaches, grapes and the famous and delectable Korla pears. Its waters are well stocked with many varieties of fish, and it supports a large area of reeds and rushes, of which some 600 million lb. (300,000 tons) are harvested each year and used for the manufacture of paper, handicrafts and building materials. Not far from its southeast bank there is a smaller saline lake that produces pure salt. ▶

Bogda Peak

Bogda Peak rises 17,860 ft. (5445 m) out of the desert in Fukang County northeast of the region's capital Urumqi to present a striking contrast of burning sands and frigid snow capped summit. Though it is not the highest peak in the Tian Mountain Range—those of Mount Tomur and Mount Hantengri are more than 3300 ft. (1000 m) higher—it has the advantage of being clearly visible from all points of the surrounding desert basins. To add to the contrast of heat and ice, its principal face has a gradient of 60 degrees, down which the snow crashes in huge avalanches, feeding more than 80 glaciers that lie in the gullies and crevices of its lower slopes. ◀

Ruins of Subashi

Not only cities and towns but splendid Buddhist monasteries crumbled into ruin when the Silk Road was overtaken by maritime transport as the main vehicle of the rich China trade. Only the jagged stumps of walls remain of the Subashi Monastery, 14 mi. (23 km) east of Kuqa County on the banks of the Tongchang River, but even these provide evidence of the lamasery's former splendor—the traces of three pagodas that overlooked the shrine halls and terraces. To the north of the ruins, a row of grottoes lines the hillside, their walls featuring carved Buddha images and inscriptions in the Kuqa language. Many relics have been unearthed in the Subashi ruins, including bronze utensils, ironware, wood carvings, murals and clay sculptures. ▼

Terra-cotta Soldiers

The Central Region (North)

For thousands of years the north central region of China has been the cradle of Chinese civilization and the nation's political powerhouse. Its Yellow River Basin is the site of one of the most important archaeological discoveries of all time—the skull of Peking Man, unearthed at Zhoukoudian in Hebei Province and regarded as evidence of human existence along the river flats no less than half a million years ago. The region's major cities, such as Luoyang, Kaifeng, Xi'an and, of course, Beijing, have been the nation's seats of power, either dynastic strongholds or imperial capitals, at various times in the vast span of history from the early Warring States to the collapse of the Manchu Qings.

It is a region immensely rich not only in history but also natural resources. Its soil is largely soft loess and exceptionally fertile. It encompasses the world's greatest man-made waterway, with the waters of the mighty Yellow River, Hai River and Yangtze River linked and harnessed by the Grand Canal—itself a monumental waterway built over a period of more than 2000 years between Hangzhou and Tianjin—to support vast croplands of wheat, cotton, corn, sorghum, peanuts, tobacco and soybeans and to provide an efficient and relatively cheap inland transport system for agricultural products and the region's huge deposits of coal, iron ore and salt.

The region embraces the loess tableland south of the Great Wall and the Central China Plain, which covers the provinces of Shaanxi, Shanxi, Henan, Hebei and Shandong. While not as physically dramatic as its neighboring regions to the northeast and northwest, it features two large mountain ranges, the Hua in the west, the central Song Range and a terrain that slopes to the east—the Yellow River tracing this gradual eastward descent as it cuts through the loess plateau and then curves through the Central Plain to empty into the Bo Sea. On its way, the river deposits vast quantities of alluvial soil, a process that gave birth to agricultural settlement along its banks 5000 to 6000 years ago but has also given the river itself the name China's Sorrow. In areas near its estuary, the alluvial deposits are so heavy that the river's bed has risen many yards above the level of the surrounding land. Despite a complex system of dykes, established over the centuries to check and tame the river's course, occasional tremendous flooding has cost thousands upon thousands of lives.

The Central Region (North) also offers a history that is just as rich—its imperial cities, dominated by the majesty and grandeur of Beijing's Forbidden City, which had been the home of 24 Chinese emperors; its temples, monasteries and other religious monuments, notably the magnificent Confucian Temple in Shandong, the Shao Lin Monastery in Song Shan and the many Buddhist temples and shrines in Heng Mountain; and its renowned archaeological treasure house, the city of Xi'an, where, among other relics, the terra-cotta army of the father of Chinese unity, the first Qin emperor, stands guard over the souls of China's imperial past.

QIAN TOMBS
乾陵

Magnificent stone lions guard the entrance to this, the burial place of Emperor Gaozong and Empress Wu of the Tang dynasty. The mausoleum, hewn out of three hills, lies at Liang Mountain in Qian County, Shaanxi. Besides the stone lions, ostriches, winged horses and soldiers that surround the tomb, there are statues of 61 leaders of regional ethnic minorities and foreign diplomats of that time. Emperor Gaozong died in AD 684, and his queen 22 years later. ▶

CHENGHUANG TEMPLE
三原縣城隍廟

This Ming dynasty temple in Sanyuan County, Shaanxi, was constructed in 1375 and is now one of the country's best-preserved examples of Ming architecture—it has kept its original design ever since it was first built. Over the centuries it has been both a place of worship, where people pray for rain, good fortune or protection, and a meeting place for merchants. In its post-imperial role, it has also served as a venue for the performing arts. ◄

YELLOW EMPEROR TOMB (HUANGDILING)

黄帝陵

The Yellow Emperor is credited with being the father of traditional Chinese medicine, the inventor of agriculture and the father of the Chinese race itself. His tomb in Qiaoshan in Huangling County, Shaanxi, was built in the Song dynasty to replace an earlier monument set up in the time of the Han. At the foot of a hill close to the tomb there are 14 cedar trees, one of which is said in legend to have been planted by the Yellow Emperor himself. A large plaque in the main hall bears the inscription First Ancestor of Humanity. ◄

FOREST OF STELAE (BEILIN)

西安碑林

In the Tang dynasty, when Xi'an was called Chang'an, the city was noted for its large collection of stone stelae, many of them featuring fine examples of early Chinese calligraphy or carvings of the Thirteen Classics of Confucian philosophy. In the year AD 904, it was decided that the entire collection should be brought under one

roof, so to speak, and a place was reserved within the city wall. But it took another 186 years for work to be completed on Xi'an's Forest of Stelae, a sprawling complex of exhibition halls, covered corridors and a pavilion, which nowadays houses more than 1000 stelaes and tomb tablets.

The exhibition virtually encompasses the history of Chinese writing, presenting the calligraphy of the Qin dynasty of the 3rd century BC, through the Tang and Song and into the Ming and final Qin reigns. In AD 1555 a powerful earthquake caused extensive damage to the halls, and the complex was rebuilt at the end of that century. Three new halls were added during the 17th and 18th centuries.

The impressive collection includes all the representative styles of Chinese calligraphy, such as the ancient official script, the highly abstract cursive script and the artistic writings of the great painter-poets, all of which became models for later students of calligraphy. Some of the stelae on display are of great historical value, such as the stela recording the introduction of Christianity into China. Another remarkable stela is a bas-relief called the Six Steeds of Zhao Mausoleum. It is in fact the tombstone of Taizong, the second emperor of the Tang dynasty, and shows the six splendid warhorses that he rode in campaigns against the northern "barbarians." ▲

GREAT WILD GOOSE PAGODA (DAYANTA)
大雁塔

This magnificent pagoda south of Xi'an was built by the Buddhist monk Tripitaka to store the sutras that he brought from India during the first flowering of the religion in China. The pagoda takes its name from a compelling incident, recorded in Tripitaka's biography, in which a flock of wild geese flew over a monastery in Magadha, a kingdom in Central India. One of them broke its wings and fell from the sky. The monks, believing that it was a Bodhisattva, buried the goose and built the pagoda in its honor.

The pagoda had only five stories when it was first built, and two others were added in the time of the Five Dynasties. It bears inscriptions by the Tang emperors Taizong and Gaozong. During their reigns it was customary for successful candidates in the civil service examinations to be entertained at the nearby Apricot Garden and then taken to Great Wild Goose Pagoda for their signing ceremony. It became a great honor for scholars to "sign at the Great Wild Goose Pagoda," and the poet Bai Juyi went one step further than that: "Of those who signed beneath the Great Wild Goose Pagoda, seventeen in all," he wrote, "I was the youngest." ▲

DRUM TOWER OF XI'AN
西安鼓樓

While Western medieval towns and forts had night-watch sentries to call the hours of the night, a large drum on the upper floor of this two-story tower in Xi'an boomed out the coming of darkness. The Drum Tower was built in 1380 in the reign of the Ming emperor Taizu and was renovated twice in the following centuries. It is remarkably well preserved and is one of the historic showpieces of a city whose name is synonymous with Chinese history. ▶

Little Wild Goose Pagoda (Xiaoyanta)

小雁塔

Located in Jianfu monastery, close to the southern gate of Xi'an, the Little Wild Goose Pagoda has a most tumultuous history—it has been struck by no less than 70 earthquakes since it was first built in the year 707 and has survived every one of them. According to the city's records, one of the tremors in 1487 was so violent that it left a split 1 ft. (a third of a meter) wide right down the middle of the tower. But 34 years later it was struck—and this time the action of the quake closed the crack. But the pagoda hasn't survived completely unscathed. It was originally 15 stories high, but earthquakes destroyed the two top floors.

In Jianfu Monastery there hangs a large bell that was cast and installed in the Ming dynasty. A beautiful poem pays tribute to its toll:

> *"Frost accompanies the grayish break of dawn,*
> *On which is painted the still dallying moon.*
> *My dream is broken by the sound of the monastery*
> *   bell,*
> *Which for ten centuries haunted the mystic air."* ▶

TOMB PAGODA OF TRIPITAKA
唐三藏墓塔

The monk Tripitaka was one of the founding fathers of the Buddhist faith in China. He was entombed in AD 669 on the slope of Shaolingyuan in what is now Changan County, Shaanxi. A monastery and pagoda were built in his memory, and when Emperor Suzong visited the site, he inscribed the characters Xing Jiao (Promotion of Religion) on a plaque, and that became the monastery's name.

A small chamber inside the 69-ft. (21-m) high five-story pagoda houses a sculpture of Tripitaka. Being a tomb, the upper stories are filled with earth. To each side of the tower there are smaller pagodas built as tombs for his principal disciples, Kuiji and Yuance. Tripitaka set out from China along the Silk Road in AD 629 on a journey in search of Buddhist scriptures from India. It took him four years. After another 16 years of study he returned to China with some 600 or more sutras, then spent another 19 years translating them into Chinese. In all, he contributed 1335 volumes to the vast bibliography of Buddhist literature in China. ▶

THE POND OF GLORIOUS PURITY (HUAQINGCHI)
華清池

One of the eight most celebrated places of natural beauty in Central China, the Pond of Glorious Purity in Shaanxi Province is also the location of a hot springs system that is steeped in history and legend. The first Qin emperor is said to have built a traveling lodge beside the springs, which are found on the slope of Mount Li in the south of Lintong County. According to folklore, on one of his visits, he encountered an immortal disguised as a common peasant woman, who, taking exception to his rather familiar behavior toward her, spat in his face. The emperor's features immediately broke out in a dread-ful skin ailment. Apologizing profusely for his indiscretions, the emperor begged her to remove the curse—and the woman revealed herself as an immortal and bathed his face in the spring, curing him as swiftly as he had been afflicted. Thereafter, the hot springs of Mount Li were known as the Immortal Hot Springs.

Another of the springs, called Hibiscus, became the trysting spot of the Tang emperor Xuanzong and his beautiful concubine Yang. The poet Bai Juyi, in his poem *Song of Everlasting Woe*, describes how the "streams of the warm fountain/Caressed her waxen limbs." ◄ ▲

Terra-cotta Soldiers

兵馬俑

The vast tomb of Emperor Qin, the first Chinese emperor to unify China's warring clans 2000 years ago, might never have been discovered since its highly skilled designers had hidden it extremely well. There is some evidence that long ago grave robbers inadvertently set fires in their search for treasures, but the tomb commissioned by Emperor Qin lay quietly 15 to 20 ft. (4.5 to 6.5 m) below the Earth's surface, covered by a roof built with layers of fiber mats followed by many feet of soil to conceal it. There is speculation that the tomb workers and supervisors were buried alive at completion to protect its secrets. In 1974 peasants near Xi'an, one of China's ancient Capitals, uncovered evidence of the tomb's fabulous terra-cotta army when digging a well. Their well excavation was over an area of the tomb with more than 8000 life-size terra-cotta warriors. The warriors' infinitely varied details of facial features, hair, dress, rank, and the horses for cavalry divisions meant that no two were alike. The figures had been fired at higher than usual temperatures for terra-cotta and were shaped by using cleverly carved molds to allow for hollow torsos, heads and arms. The legs were solid terra-cotta needed to support each figure's overall weight of up to 600 lb. (300 kg). Experts believe this terra-cotta army is only a small part of the buried treasures of Emperor Qin's tomb since it lies approximately less than a mile (1000 m) east of the main tomb. The main entrance to the tomb has still not been located even to this day. ▼ ▶

Hua Mountain
華山

Hua Mountain (Western Sacred Mountain), lying south of Huayin County in Shaanxi, is another dramatic beauty spot that for centuries has been a symbol of the Chinese reverence and delight in nature. The names alone that have been given to its various peaks and viewpoints bear tribute to a feeling that goes beyond mere popularity. Its name translates into Great Flower Mountain; its highest peak, Luoyan (7260 ft. or 2200 m), is Descending Wild Duck Peak. Another of its summits, Jade Girl (Yunu) Peak, commemorates the daughter of a Zhou dynasty prince who renounced her aristocracy to come to live on Hua Mountain with a flute player and recluse named Xiaoshi. Nearby, Gold Lock (Jinsuo) Pass leads to Lotus Blossom (Lianhua) Peak, and another path climbs to Facing Sun (Zhaoyang) Peak, where there is a terrace built for the viewing of the sunrise. East of Zhaoyang, Immortal's Palm Cliff celebrates a legend in which a river god called Juling created the course of the Yellow River, leaving a palm print in the rock to remind mortal beings of the cataclysmic event. ▲ ▶

JIN SHRINE
晉祠

J in Shrine, a complex of 100 or so halls, shrines and pavilions, has a history so vast that the exact date of its construction is still a matter of conjecture. It is claimed, however, in the classic *Shi Jing Zhu*, written more than 1400 years ago, to have been built in memory of Shuyu, the second son of Emperor Wu of Zhou (1122–1115 BC). It has been renovated several times since then. Set in a beautifully landscaped garden of trees and streams, it offers some of the most interesting and valuable examples of different dynastic architecture found anywhere in China, along with several clay images that are considered masterpieces of Chinese art. ▶

Three Springs

In the Jin Shrine in Taiyuan City in Shanxi, there are three springs, two of which flow intermittently and one, called Nanlao (Loath to Get Old), that gushes constantly and maintains the same 63°F (17°C) temperature all year-round. A pagoda nearby called Water Mother Mansion refers to a legend that has also sprung from the bore. It appears that when Water Mother was a young maiden, she had to fetch water over a long and tiring distance each day. A mysterious stranger gave her a whip and told her to store it in her water jar, and to take it out only when she wanted water. When her domineering mother-in-law saw that she was cheating on her chore, she confiscated the magic whip—and the jar has overflowed with water ever since. ▼

Huayan Monastery
山西華嚴寺

Construction of Huayan Monastery in southwest Datong, Shanxi, began in the Liao dynasty (AD 916–1125) and reflects the superstitions of the Khitan tribespeople who swept down from the north to seize China's central plain. The halls and shrines all face the east to conform with the Khitan worship of the sun and their fear of evil influences from other points of the compass. The monastery was renovated in the Ming period of the 15th century and divided into upper and lower terraces. The upper monastery, which contains the principal hall, Daxiongbaodian, built in the Jin dynasty (1115–1234), features 31 clay sculptures of Liao-period Bodhisattvas.

The Great Hall of the Upper Temple of the Huayan complex was rebuilt in 1140, then renovated during the Ming reign—and has been given additional touches right up to the turn of this century. The murals of the main hall, 9,688 sq. ft. (900 sq. m) of them, depict the life of Sakyamuni Buddha, images of arhats, thousand-eye Bodhisattvas and the fierce pantheon of Chinese gods that were painted in 1875 to 1908 by the artist Dong An. Among the many relics in the shrine hall are five gilded Maitreya Buddhas seated on lotus pedestals and more garish statues of 20 Heavenly Guards. ▲ ▶

YUNGANG CAVES
雲岡石窟

The Yungang grottoes are located 10 mi. (16 km) west of Datong in Shanxi. Carved into the northern slope of Mount Wuzhou more than 1500 years ago, they are rated as one of the three most significant examples of Buddhist cave art in China. Ancient records indicate that the caves were situated close to a community of Buddhist monasteries flourishing in the Liao and Jin periods. There are now 53 caves in all, covering almost 0.6 mi. (1 km) of the cliff face and containing over 51,000 Buddhist images. Three different periods and styles of Buddhist art are represented. Stupas of innumerable forms and variations are found in the eastern caves, while the western caves contain figures that bear the influence of Indian art. The central caves, the largest and earliest to be carved, contain images that are said to have been modeled on the rulers of the northern Wei dynasty of AD 386–534. Each of the five grottoes (numbers 16–20) contains a statue of Buddha at least 43 ft. (13 m) tall. The one in grotto number 19 (far right) is the most imposing, while the gigantic Buddha sitting outside grotto number 20 (below), with a dignified but faintly amused expression, is said to be carved in typical northern Wei style. ▼ ▶

Grotto Number 13

Of all the grottoes in Yungang, Grottoes numbers 9 and 13 are known as the Wuhua Caves and are noted for the ornate and brightly colored flower-and-plant motifs, altars, sculptured musicians and instruments added there by artists of the Qing dynasty. The most commanding relic of this sec-

tion is a huge cross-legged Buddha, 43 ft. (13 m) high, reposing in grotto number 13 and representing a sculptural style that is unique in Yungang. Between its right arm and thigh stands a much smaller statue of a "four-armed strong-man." ▼

Grotto Number 5

Another grotto that has drawn a great deal of attention is grotto number 5. Linked to grotto number 6, which is the largest in Yungang, this grotto has a four-tiered wooden structure decorating its entrance.

Forming the centerpiece inside is a 56-ft. (17-m) high sitting Buddha, an image that was probably first sculpted in the art style of the northwest region of China during the Tang dynasty, then remodeled according to the Han school with loose-fitting robes and a long flowing sash. This is one of the more opulent of the Yungang Caves. Its walls are packed with altars and bas-relief images that reach up to cover the interior of the domed ceiling. The arch doorway is flanked by a Buddha sitting under the bodhi tree. The bas-relief images on the ceiling are renowned for the beauty of their artistic design. So are the ones found in grotto number 9 (right). ▽ ▷

WUTAI MOUNTAIN
五台山

Thirty-nine monasteries lie within the bounds of Wutai, one of the five mountain ranges regarded as Buddhist or Taoist holy places in China. Wutai's five hills are situated in the northeast corner of Wutai County, Shanxi, and their slopes, running with clear streams and covered with lush meadows, stand out in contrast with the generally arid terrain around them. Wutai Mountain was declared a holy place during the East Han dynasty in the years AD 58–75 when an Indian monk visited the region, claimed the mountain as a fitting place in which to worship the Manjusri Bodhisattva, and petitioned the emperor to build a monastery there. ▲

SAKYA PAGODA
佛宮寺釋迦塔

This magnificent 900-year-old five-story pagoda in the Fugong Monastery in Ying County, Shanxi, is the oldest and largest wooden pagoda in China and one of very few ancient wooden structures to have survived earthquakes, fire and other ravages of time, apparently none the worse for wear. Eight-sided with six eaves, its interior construction is quite ingenious—it actually has not five but nine floors inside. Among its most treasured relics is a collection of colored Buddha images printed with woodblocks on silk, dating back to the Liao dynasty. A gilded statue of Sakyamuni Buddha, 36 ft. (11 m) tall, towers over the altar on the ground floor. ▶

FLYING RAINBOW PAGODA
廣勝上寺飛虹塔

The ornate green-and-polychrome tile work and general design of this pagoda offer visitors little doubt that its name has something to do with color. And color is the dominant theme of the Flying Rainbow Pagoda of the Guangsheng Monastery northeast of Xi'an. The eaves of its first three stories are packed with exquisitely carved and painted Buddha niches, Bodhisattvas, animals and flowers. Elsewhere, the walls of the rear hall of the monastery's lower section are filled with strikingly colored murals that look down on Yuan dynasty sculptures of the Amitabha, Maitreya and Sakyamuni Buddhas and various Bodhisattvas and deities. Flying Rainbow Pagoda was first constructed in the Han dynasty and, like many Chinese Buddhist landmarks, rebuilt by the industrious Ming. ◄

CHONGSHAN MONASTERY
崇善寺

This monastery in the southeastern district of Taiyuan in Shanxi is thought to have been built during the transition from the Tang to Song dynasties. In 1381 its principal Dabei Hall was added by the third son of the founding emperor of the Ming dynasty, dedicated to the memory of his mother. Inside the prayer hall stands a gilded thousand-hand, thousand-eye Bodhisattva Avalokitesvara with 11 faces, and other Bodhisattva images, all of them standing 28 ft. (8.5 m) tall. A large collection of Song, Yuan and Ming editions of the sutras is kept here, along with a most valuable volume, which was printed in 1231, in the reign of the Southern Song ruler, Lizong. ►

XUANKONG MONASTERY
懸空寺

The dramatic Xuankong Monastery, which clings to the face of a sheer cliff south of Hunyuan County in Shanxi, is—not surprisingly—called the Hanging in Air Monastery. It is said to have been built in the early 6th century and renovated several times since, each new rebuilding project remaining faithful to the original daring design in which some of the halls and pavilions are only supported by timber piles driven into the rock. A network of narrow paths cut into the cliff face connects the monastery's two principal halls and some 40 other buildings. This astonishing group of buildings has stood firm against centuries of erosion and earthquakes, and its spectacular setting has inspired many poets to write its praise.

▲

XUANZHONG MONASTERY
玄中寺

This 1500-year-old monastery west of Xijiao City in Shanxi had its heyday in the Mongol Yuan dynasty when nearly 40 other monasteries in the region came under its control. It was also regarded as the "ancestral institution" of several eminent monks who promoted the Pure Land sect of Buddhism there—a school of Mahayana

in which Nirvana was interpreted as a magnificent paradise or Pure Land in the west—and later introduced it to Japan. Some of the remaining shrines and halls of Xuanzhong Monastery belong to the Song era, others to Yuan and Ming, but the Ten-Thousand Buddha Hall and Thousand Buddha Chamber are more recent additions of the Qing dynasty. ▼

PINGYAO CITY
平遙古城

Pingyao City, historically one of the first cities in northern China, is famous as a walled city with many traditional dwellings, government offices, shops, and temples dating to the Ming and Qing dynasties that are still intact. Zhenguo Temple and Shuanling Temple house painted statues dating from 400–1000 years old. At its prime, Pingyao City's strategic location on the banks of the Yellow River in Shanxi gave it power as a transportation hub and commercial center. It was established during the Western Zhou dynasty (1100–711 BC), but the old city wall seen today was recent by comparison, built in 1370 during the Ming dynasty. There is a long-held belief in the area that the rammed earth and brick wall in the shape of a tortoise is key to the 2700-year history of Pingyao, since the tortoise is one of the symbols of longevity in Chinese culture. The city gates on the east and west sides are compared to the legs of the tortoise, and the south and north gates are the head and tail of the animal. Two wells outside the south gate are like the eyes, and the streets and lanes seem to suggest the pattern of the tortoise's shell.

▼ ▶

LONGMEN CAVES
龍門石窟

The third of the three greatest Buddhist grottoes in China, these caves were dug around the year AD 493 on the bank of the Yi River, south of Luoyang City in Henan. Since then, the cliff has been literally honey-combed with grottoes—over 2000 of them containing 100,000 sculptured images, 40 stone towers and 3600 stone carvings and inscribed stelae and plaques. These stelae include 30 that feature a variety of styles of calligraphy known as the Twenty Types at Longmen. Most of the caves date back to the Northern Wei (AD 386–534) and Tang (618–907) eras and feature sculptures of emperors, princes and nobles of those times, alongside the Buddhas.

At the southern end of Longmen, there is a temple named Fengxian. Its construction began in AD 672 during the reign of the Tang emperor, Gaozong, and it took four years to complete this, the largest of the open-air grottoes at Longmen. A donation from the Empress Wu helped the project along. The huge cavern, 115 ft. (35 m) long and 98 ft. (30 m) wide, features nine large Buddha statues, the tallest one standing nearly 59 ft. (18 m) high. It has pronounced Han Chinese Buddha features, with long drooping ears and expressive eyes, and its robes are voluminous. In the north wall of the cave, there are statues of a Heavenly Guard and a strongman, both well preserved. (bottom) The guard supports a pagoda in the palm of its hand, and one of its feet rests heavily on a demon.

WHITE HORSE MONASTERY (BAIMASI)

河南白馬寺

This is the oldest Buddhist institution in China, built in AD 68 just east of what is now the city of Luoyang. And it is linked with the very birth of the Buddhist faith in China. It is said that in AD 64 the Han emperor Ming had a dream in which a golden Buddha flew around his palace. He saw this as a heavenly message, and responded by sending two emissaries to India to seek Buddhist enlightenment. Two Indian monks were also invited to visit China, and they turned up via the Silk Route with Buddhist sutras "carried by white horses." White Horse Monastery was built to celebrate the event.

The monastery has been renovated and expanded over the centuries, and its present architecture is the result of extensive work carried out in 1713 in the reign of Emperor Kangxi. The complex is smaller than the original—which accommodated more than 1000 monks—and has, of course, lost its early Indian influences. However, there are still some faint traces of Indian design in its Qingliang Terrace, Ganlu Well and Sutra-Burning Terrace. To the east of the monastery stands the Qiyun Pagoda (opposite), built in 1175—a 12-tiered brick tower, 79 ft. (24 m) high, which has weathered the centuries surprisingly well. The graves of the two Indian monks in whose honor the monastery was built lie near the main gate. ▲ ▶

SHAOLIN MONASTERY
少林寺

This monastery, built in the time of the Northern Wei dynasty northwest of Dengfeng County in Henan, is considered to be the birthplace of Zen Buddhism. It was constructed in tribute to Bodhidharma, the founder of Zen, who was reputed to be the supreme champion of the martial arts—he taught his disciples the principles of boxing and unarmed combat—and was said to be so light of weight that he crossed the Yangtze River on a flimsy reed. The monastery's heyday was in the Sui and Tang dynasties when it included no less than 5000 shrines, halls, pagodas and pavilions. Almost all of these have since been demolished, and all that remain of the principal buildings are the Bodhidharma Pavilion, Thousand Buddha Hall, White Robe Hall and Bodhisattva Kitigarbha Hall.

The White Robe Hall, built in the late Qing dynasty, features wall murals depicting various movements and major events of the martial arts, including the epic Thirteen Monks Rescuing the King of Tang. It is said that the monks, already skilled exponents of kung fu, joined forces to serve with distinction as retainers of the first Tang emperor. One of the favors they received for their loyalty and protection was permission to build a fortified camp at the monastery.

Some of these monks are buried in the Forest of Stupas (below), featuring some 220 stupas of different architectural styles, that lies to the west of the monastery. In the Thousand Buddha Hall, more evidence of their ancient discipline can be seen—rounded hollows worn in the tiled floor by the constant training that went on over the centuries.

FAN PAGODA
繁塔

This hexagonal brick pagoda was built in Kaifeng in the year 977 (Song dynasty) to celebrate the arrival of the Fan family to take up residence in the city. Though otherwise undistinguished, each of its bricks contains a round niche with a carved Buddha in it. At that time, Kaifeng was a great Song dynasty metropolis called Bianjing, and it enjoyed wealth, refinement and expansion until northern tribal pressure on the Song rule led to the dynasty's collapse and the rise of the Jin dynasty, based in Bianjing on the site of modern Kaifeng, Henan Province. Kaifeng has suffered a great deal over the centuries from the calamitous flooding of the nearby Yellow River. Many of its most historic sites were badly damaged or destroyed in the worst floods of 1642, when defenders of the Ming dynasty deliberately breached the dykes protecting the city. ◄

GUANLIN
關林

Towering out of farmlands 4 mi. (7 km) from Luoyang, Guanlin is said to have been the burial place of General Guan Yu of the Three Kingdoms period that followed the Han dynasty. Noted as a brave and efficient soldier, Guan Yu was one of three generals who together established the western kingdom of Shu Han, in what is now modern Sichuan, during the collapse of Han rule. Eventually, one of the three competing kingdoms, the Wei in the north of China, overcame and annexed Shu Han to establish the Wei dynasty. This order was followed by the Jin dynasty, which ruled China for a short period, and some 20 other dynastic orders in which the Han Chinese lost power to various non-Chinese tribal groups such as the Xiongnu, Qiang, Xianbi Badi and Jie. It was not until AD 589, some 250 years after the fall of the Han dynasty, that the reins of power were wrested back into Chinese hands in the Sui dynasty of Emperor Yang Jian. ▶

STAR-WATCHING TERRACE

觀星台

This Star-Watching Terrace is the oldest of 27 observatories built throughout China during the reign of the Mongol Yuans. At that time Chinese astronomy had been adapted from the Arabic system and was used in conjunction with the theories and calculations of traditional Chinese astronomers and geomancers to maintain a calendar foretelling the positions of the heavenly bodies and the timing of the seasons—an essential function in the agricultural society and a crucial responsibility of the emperor himself through the astronomical bureau of his Board of Rites in Beijing. In 1610 the system got it wrong, miscalculating an eclipse by several hours, and that gave the Portuguese Jesuits in the imperial court an opportunity to revise the Chinese calendar with modern European methods and to curry added imperial favor for Christianity in China. ◀

Iron Pagoda (Tieta)

鐵塔

Built in 1049 during the Song dynasty, the Iron Pagoda is so called because of the metallic color of its tiles. It is a replica of an earlier wooden structure that was destroyed by fire, and the columns, brackets and rafters decorated with 28 different kinds of tiles faithfully reproduce the details of the original wooden structure. This is an early example of prefabricated construction in the history of Chinese architecture.

Standing more than 160 ft. (50 m) and 13 stories tall, the pagoda's surface is covered with carved motifs that include flying apsaras, descending dragons, unicorns, lions and Bodhisattvas. Built on rocks on the top of Yi Mountain, the pagoda has firm foundations. The special stairway on the upper part of the pagoda binds the outer walls tightly to the core pillar, thus strengthening the entire structure. ◄

Dragon Pavilion (Longting)

龍亭

Looking almost like a pavilion of Beijing's Forbidden City, Dragon Pavilion lies between two ornamental lakes in Kaifeng. It was built in the final Qing dynasty on what is thought to have been the site of the palace of the Northern Song emperor. The pavilion stands on a raised brick dais with a double roof, yellow-glazed tiles and red pillars and walls. Among its relics is a cube decorated with carved dragons, which is thought to have been the Song emperor's throne. Its two nearby lakes are called Yang and Pan, and they have become part of the local folklore. Yang is a clear lake and is named after a family who are said to have lived beside the lake and were noted for their loyalty to the emperor. The Pan lake is muddy, reflecting, it is said, the treachery of the disloyal Pans who also lived on its shore. ▲

Cangyan Mountain

蒼岩山

Cangyan Mountain in Jingxing County, Hebei, is an extension of the Taihang Mountain Range.

It is noted for its harmonious blending of nature and art. Exquisitely designed monasteries and studios are interspersed among the foliage of pines and white sandalwood, rugged rocks and cascading streams.

In a precarious but well-protected setting, Fuqing Monastery clings to the upper ledge of one of the mountain's sheer cliff faces.

The curved tile roof of the monastery is typical of tradi-tional Chinese architecture. It evolved in the Song dynasty, an age in which art and architecture flourished, and became more and more flamboyant over the ensuing centuries. Ornate and sometimes garish ornaments were placed at either end of the roof ridge, and animal sculptures on the eaves to ward off evil spirits. Roofs were originally thatched, but were gradually tiled with glazed terra cotta or porcelain in the distinctive semi-cylindrical design that is said to have been based on split bamboo. ▲

Qiaolou Hall

Originally built at the end of the 6th century, Qiaolou Hall, the main building of the Fuqing Monastery, was reconstructed at the start of the Qing dynasty. The decorative ceramic figurines and animals placed on the green and yellow tiled roof and the painting in Su style on the columns and beams are typical of the architectural design in the early Qing period.

The hall perches on a single-arched stone bridge high over a deep ravine. The bridge is 49 ft. (15 m) long and 30 ft. (9 m) wide. Looking down the gorge from the hall, the trees and grass below appear to be a sea of green. The sky above seems so close that one can almost touch the floating clouds.

The gateway to the monastery, at the top of a long flight of steps on the north side of Cangyan Mountain, bears a welcoming couplet: "The hall has no lamps, the moon illuminates it; the gateway is unlocked, the clouds seal it." ▼

Zhaozhou Bridge
趙州橋

Also known as Anji Bridge, this is unquestionably one of the world's great masterpieces of bridge-building technology—and it was constructed nearly 1400 years ago. The Zhaozhou Bridge, built between AD 605 and 618, is single-spanned and more than 160 ft. (50 m) long. It is celebrated not only for its long span and for the incomparable beauty and economy of its design but also for the innovative engineering of its segmental arches.

Two pairs of segmental arches stand on the main arch in the spandrels to reduce the load of the spandrel masonry and provide an overflow for floodwaters. It was not until the 14th century that this "open spandrel" technique was adopted in European bridge building, 700 years after the construction of Zhaozhou. Despite constant use for many centuries, the bridge has weathered well without major renovation. Some of the original posts and beautifully carved panels of the balustrades were lost over the centuries, crumbling away and falling into the river, and in 1953 some of these were dug out of the mud of the riverbed and reinstalled. ▲

LUGOU BRIDGE

盧溝橋

Marco Polo called this "the finest bridge in the world," which it undoubtedly was when it was completed in the year 1193. In those days, the Chinese were nearly 1000 years ahead of the Europeans, and indeed the rest of the world, in many fields of engineering and science. The bridge was repaired in the Ming dynasty, and then, after having been badly damaged by floods, was rebuilt in 1698 (the 37th year of the Qing emperor Kangxi). Now it remains a fine and remarkably strong structure as well as a unique architectural relic.

Spanning the Yongding River southwest of Beijing, Lugou Bridge is 873 ft. (266 m) long with 11 arches. It was designed so that it could withstand the force of wind and ice. However, even more famous than its design are the stone carvings on the bridge. There are 485 vividly carved stone lions, all in different postures, forming a kind of ceremonial guard along the balustrades—in fact, there are so many of them that the phrase "stone lions of Lugou Bridge" has come to mean anything of which there are "so many that one loses count." ▼ ▶

THE ANCIENT PALACES (FORBIDDEN CITY)

故宫

Better known all over the world as Beijing's Forbidden City, the Ancient Palaces were the residence and political nerve center of the emperors of the Ming and succeeding Manchu Qing dynasties, and the hotbed of intrigue among their huge courts. The original palaces, which took 15 years to build, were started in 1406 by the third emperor of the Ming dynasty, Chengzu, when he moved the imperial capital to Beijing. The complex, the largest surviving cluster of wooden buildings on such a scale in the world, has since played a central role in the most momentous phases of contemporary Chinese history—the wealth, power and glory of the Ming, the Manchu triumph of the Qing dynasty, then its gradual decay in the face of foreign pressure and incursion, and finally the complete collapse of the dynastic order. After the fall of the Manchus and establishment of the short-lived Chinese republic, the Forbidden City fell into disrepair but was restored in the 1950s according to its original plans—the spirits of 24 great and not-so-great divine rulers of China's immense past still facing south, according to ancient Chinese geomancy, and their people facing north in obeisance.

Wumen

This gigantic terrace, on which stands the Five Phoenix Mansions, is the main front entrance to the Forbidden City. Wumen (Midday Gate) is where the emperors issued edicts, had miscreant mandarins publicly flogged and presided over the execution of common criminals sharp at noon. Built in 1420 and rebuilt in 1647, it is actually five gateways, the central one reserved for the emperor's carriages. Once inside, visitors and emissaries proceeded to the Taihe Hall, where the rulers conducted state ceremonies and political business, or to the Baohe Hall, which was the setting for state banquets and, at one time, the examination hall for civil service candidates. Another mansion, Zhonghe Hall, was where the emperors studied briefing papers before attending meetings in the Taihe Hall. An inner section of the palaces, north of Baohe Hall, included the emperor's living quarters and Imperial Garden. ▲

Corner Pavilion

The Forbidden City was so called because the common people were forbidden to enter it, and observation and security towers Placed at each corner of the 1.6-million-sq. ft. (150,000-sq.-m) palace grounds made certain that all but

the aristocracy were kept out. These pavilions were based on the designs of the Yellow Crane and Prince Teng mansions of the Song dynasty, and today their complex and extravagant roof structures are regarded as yet another masterpiece of traditional architecture. ▼

Qianqing Hall

This Qing dynasty reception and banqueting hall also served a crucial role in the security and harmony of the dynastic order. It was where the Qing emperors chose their successors. From the time of Emperor Yongzheng, who assumed the throne in 1723, it was the custom for each ruler to write the name of his intended successor on two pieces of paper—one to be kept in his personal possession and the other secreted behind a plaque bearing the inscription "upright and bright." (above) Upon the emperor's death, his closest ministers would compare the two names, and if they tallied, they announced the new ruler. More than 40 mansions surround the Qianqing Hall, some of them containing the emperor's crown and robes of office and books and artworks; others being places where he held audiences with his chief scholars and advisers; and still others being used as reading rooms, medical consulting rooms and living quarters for the imperial servants, maids, concubines and palace eunuchs. ▲

THE SUMMER PALACE
颐和园

The powerful and ruthless Empress Dowager (Cixi), the last real dynastic ruler of China, built the Summer Palace in 1888 on the site of a previous palace and garden that had dated from the Jin dynasty. The project has since been regarded as something of an extravagant folly. For one thing, the empress appropriated much of the cost of it, some 24 million taels of silver, from funds set up to modernize the Chinese navy—and was soon to see the navy, or fleets of magnificent but obsolete and outgunned war junks, suffer a humiliating defeat under the guns and rockets of a British iron-hulled steam-paddle warship brought from England to smash open the doors to free trade in China. As for the Summer Palace itself, Allied Forces gutted and plundered it two years after it had been completed, and a subsequent rebuilding project only added to its vast cost. Nowadays its lake, gardens, shrines and pavilions are open to the public, along with another symbol of the empress Dowager's stubborn extravagance, the giant Marble Boat on Kunming Lake, a stone replica of a showboat paddle steamer.

A bronze pavilion, called Pavilion of Precious Clouds, is another feature of the Summer Palace. It was cast in 1750 and reaches a height of nearly 26 ft. (8 m) and weighs more than 200 tons. ▲ ▶

The Long Gallery

This corridor, 2400 ft. (728 m) long, follows the line of the northern bank of Kunming Lake and is designed to reflect its special blend of architecture and nature in the still waters around it. Its ceiling is also painted with some 8000 "still life" compositions of flowers and scenes from famous Chinese stories and legends, and for this reason it is also called the Picture Corridor. Halfway along the gallery lies the empress Dowager's opulent Palace Which Dispels Clouds; further along stands the beautiful Listening to Orioles Hall (Tingliguan); and at the end of the corridor the garish white Marble Boat reflects the sudden twist of refinement to vulgarity that took place in the empress Dowager's reign. ▶

Kunming Lake

A number of streams from the western districts of Beijing, including one called Jade Spring Mountain, were channeled by engineers of the Yuan dynasty to form the great lake of the Summer Palace. The Qing emperor, Qianlong, gave it its name when he refurbished a Ming dynasty palace and temple, the Duabao Pagoda, to celebrate his mother's 60th birthday. Later, the empress Dowager added much of the rest of the construction around the lake, including the Palace Which Dispels Clouds, which she built to celebrate her own birthday. ▼

TEMPLE OF HEAVEN
天壇

Tiantan, the Temple of Heaven, in the southwestern corner of Beijing, is an ensemble of shrines and was once the venue for the most important imperial rites—prayers for good harvest, sacrifices to the gods and royal ancestors and communion with the heavens. Built in 1420 (the 18th year of the reign of the Ming emperor Yongle), the building is part of a series of four temples in Beijing representing the firmament, the others being the Temple of the Sun, the Temple of the Earth and the Temple of the Moon. The buildings are spaced out over an area of more than 29.4 million sq. ft. (2,700,000 sq. m), and altogether took 14 years to build.

The Temple of Heaven consists of two main structures linked by a 1188-ft.-long (360-m-long) bridge. It is regarded as the most remarkable architectural composition, in which mathematical balance and economy of design have achieved an almost overwhelming majesty. It is also a masterpiece of acoustics, its most novel feature being a circular wall of polished bricks in Huangqiong House (Imperial Vault of Heaven), where echoes run clearly from one end to another, giving it the name Echo Wall (bottom, opposite). This hall also contains sacred ancestral tablets, as well as those dedicated to the gods of rain, the sun, the moon, the stars, dawn, the wind, thunder and lightning. When Western troops invaded Beijing in 1860 and 1900, the Temple of Heaven suffered serious damage, and it was not until 1918 that the temple was repaired and reopened to the public. ▲

Qiniandian

This, the Temple for Praying for a Good Harvest, shown at far left and with a detail of its domed ceiling (left), dominates the Temple of Heaven from the top of three concentric terraces fenced with carved white marble balustrades. It is where the emperor came each year at the first full moon for fertility rites that go back to the distant beginnings of Chinese history. At the winter solstice he would also mount the three terraces of the Circular Sacrificial Altar where, after much prayer and traditional clay pipe music, a young bullock would be sacrificed to the gods. As such, the emperor was the vital conduit between the teeming Chinese society and the spiritual forces that ruled much of its existence. Though sometimes a harsh and despotic ruler himself, he was also servant of two masters—acting as the vehicle through which the people's fears and wishes were made known to the heavenly deities, and a kind of human lightning rod for bolts of good fortune or retribution from on high. ◄

NORTHSEA (BEIHAI) PARK

北海公園

For more than 1000 years the North Sea Park—as mundane as its name may be—was the royal garden of successive dynasties that included the Liao, Jin, Yuan and Ming. It covers an area of 7.6 million sq. ft. (700,000 sq. m), and among its beautifully landscaped gardens, hillocks and pools there are two particular artistic attractions. One, the famous Nine Dragon Wall (top right), is a 86-ft.-long (26-m-long) ceramic monument made up of 424 seven-colored glazed tiles depicting nine dragons in high relief on each side. The other showpiece is the White Stupa (or Dagoba), which is a prime example of Tibetan Buddhist architecture. Built in 1651, it was badly damaged by earthquakes in 1679 and 1731. ▼ ▶

Little Garden of Qianlong

Nature and the architect's vision have blended splendidly to create this garden within a garden, originally called Jingxinzhai, or Quiet Mind Studio, on the northern shore of Beihai in Beijing. It features elaborate formations of rocks from Lake Tai in artificial hills and craggy shorelines around the garden's lotus and lily-covered ponds, and a series of peaceful pavilions and water bowers. Constructed in 1758, the Little Garden was completely renovated in 1913 after the fall of the dynastic order and the setting up of the Chinese republic, and was used as a reception venue for foreign diplomats. ◄

YUANMING YUAN
圓明園

The ruins of Yuan Ming Yuan, the imperial gardens of the Summer Palace outside Beijing, are still a famous destination in China even though few traces of its magnificent beauty remain today. In the past, the gardens were the home of the emperor and his court from the beginning of each Chinese lunar New Year in early spring until autumn. For over 150 years the gardens, bridges, pagodas and residences were the pet project of emperors who based their design on well-known scenic spots in China and other famous garden designs. The area for the gardens was already blessed with an abundance of natural springs and hills, but that was just the raw material for the creation of a fairytale landscape that exemplified the imperial desire to have all the beauty of China belong within the emperor's garden walls. Rivers, waterfalls, lakes and islands dotted the transformed landscape. The theme of each special garden site was created to represent China's cherished artistic, literary and philosophical concepts that the emperor then had the privilege of naming. The finest materials went in to the building of the garden's exquisite architecture. These marvelous structures were furnished from the vast imperial collections of art, antiques and books. As contact with the west began to influence imperial taste, western buildings and art objects were added to Yuan Ming Yuan. The gardens represented the culmination of 2000 years of Chinese garden design. Sadly, the weakened Qing dynasty in the second half of the 19th century was unable to protect China, and as foreign powers vied in Beijing for the rich spoils, the imperial gardens were eventually set on fire and the treasures looted. For many years thereafter, even in a disastrous state of ruin, the gardens inspired poetry describing its tragic beauty. ◄ ▼

Yonghe Palace
雍和宫

The Qing emperor Yongzheng lived in this complex first as a prince and later as emperor, using parts of the premises for the practice of Tibetan Buddhism. When the emperor died, his coffin was lodged here, and the green roof tiles were replaced by yellow ones, whereby the place was officially elevated to the rank of a palace for housing Yongzheng's image and for the ancestral worship of the royal Qing house. The palace was presented to the lamas by Emperor Qianlong in 1744 and turned into a lamasery, and it stands today as the largest and one of the best-preserved Buddhist institutions in China. In the five halls that make up the monastery, valuable Buddhist images in bronze and stone stand alongside rare relics of the Yellow Sect of Tibetan Buddhism, including ancient copies of the Tripitaka sutras. Its walls contain many colorful murals of Buddhist stories and Buddha images. The many side rooms also house valuable collections of Buddhist scriptures and writings in mathematics, medicine, astronomy, and geography. ▲ ▶

Buddha Tooth Sarira Pagoda
佛牙舍利塔

According to the Buddhist chronicles, when Sakyamuni Buddha died, two particles of Sarira (Sheli) from his teeth were found in the cremation ashes. One of them was taken to the Lion Country or what is now Sri Lanka, and the other was saved by the monk Faxian. It was installed as a highly sacred relic in a temple that stood where the Sarira Pagoda has since been built.

Sarira, a word derived from Sanskrit, is the technical term for what is recognized as the highest and most developed state of spiritual life—the state in which the vital physical juices are transformed into small brilliant "jewels" that are found in the ashes after the cremation fires have done their work. The name is used also simply to designate a relic, and pagodas and shrines in which Sheli jewels are kept are held in high esteem. ▲

FRAGRANT HILL (XIANGSHAN)
香山

his scenic park northwest of Beijing is a location that has been favored by imperial dynasties since the 12th century when it was chosen as an imperial hunting ground. Pavilions, temples and summer retreats for the imperial family have graced the park, but time, changes in fashion and the destruction of much imperial property in the late 19th century by foreign powers have conspired to remove many of the structures built in the park over its long history. The brilliant autumn foliage of the smoke trees that cover the hills to the west of the park has long made the park a popular destination. For the hardy admirers of nature, winter also is a favorite time to take in the beauty of snow-covered hills.

There are a number of temples in the park, including the Temple of Brilliance, a copy of a Tibetan temple. The delightful Glazed Tile Pagoda has bronze bells that tinkle in the wind and hang from the eaves of each of its seven stories. A small garden within the park was once the site of the Summer Palace. The semicircular pool surrounded by a covered walkway is similar to the original that once decorated the grounds of the Summer Palace. ▲

Glazed Pagoda of Xiangshan

This beautiful green pagoda is eight-sided and seven-tiered but only 33 ft. (10 m) tall. It stands in Xiangshan Park in Beijing and was built in typical Qing dynasty fashion, with a combination of stone tiles and wooden corridors and 56 bronze wind bells tinkling from its many eaves. It is the only structure to survive inside the Zhao Temple, which was built in 1780 (the 45th year of the reign of the Qing emperor Qianlong) in the Tibetan style of architecture, and served as a guesthouse to the sixth Panchen lama when he visited Beijing. The pagoda, which lies to the west of it, is now regarded as the emblem of this complex. ▼

Shifangpujue Monastery

Located on the southern slope of Shouan Hill just outside Beijing, this monastery was first built in the Tang dynasty in the 7th century and rebuilt in 1734 (the 12th year of the Qing emperor Yongzheng). It is also called the Sleeping Buddha Monastery, because it houses a reclining statue of Buddha. The main feature of this symmetrically designed monastery is the Hall of the Sleeping Buddha, where a bronze image of Sakyamuni lies in an apparent state of Nirvana. The statue, cast in 1321 in the Yuan dynasty, is more than 17 ft. (5 m) long and depicts Sakyamuni speaking with his disciples about his impending departure from all earthly things. Lying on one side, with his right hand pitched against his head, the Buddha is the very picture of ease and calm, attended by disciples represented here as 12 clay statues standing behind him. ▲

Biyun Monastery

When Buddhism first took root in China, its architecture naturally followed the style of that of its birthplace, India. But almost all early Chinese construction was of wood, and the evidence of whole periods of history was destroyed by fire. Through a combination of reconstruction and its own artistic development, Han Chinese architecture soon dominated the design of religious and public buildings. A group of white marble pagodas remains, however, as a striking example of early Indian design in the Biyun Monastery on the eastern slope of Fragrant Hill or Xiangshan, in Beijing. The tallest is 13-tiered and 116 ft. (35 m) high and is decorated with Tibetan Buddhist themes in bas-relief. ▶

MING TOMBS (SHISANLING)
明十三陵

Ranking with the Forbidden City and the Great Wall as one of the most renowned monuments to Chinese imperial history, the Ming Tombs lie in the shadow of Tianshou Mountain 31 mi. (50 km) north of Beijing. They were built as mausoleums for 13 emperors of the Ming dynasty from the reign of Chengzue to Sizong, covering a period of more than 200 years from 1409 to 1644. The approach to the tombs alone is monumental—an 11-story white marble memorial archway with five gates and six pillars is the main entrance; beyond it stands the Dahong Gate (Red Main Gate) with red walls and yellow roof tiles; and beyond that lies a wide 4-mi (7-km) Road of the Gods (top opposite) lined with large stone sculptures of lions, camels, elephants, unicorns and horses and statues of court officials in the ceremonial dress, each slightly bowed in a gesture of respect. The tombs of the emperors and their consorts are found in the Baocheng (Precious) City, each surrounded by a red wall and each containing a particular stone tablet that, unlike the others, has nothing inscribed upon it—symbolizing the infinite beneficence of the imperial rulers. ◀

Chang Tomb (Changling)

No other tomb ranks in size and grandeur with the Chang Tomb, built in 1413 for the emperor Yongle. Its Lingen Hall stands on a 10-ft.- (3-m-) high white marble podium. It covers an area of 20,452 sq. ft (1900 sq. m) and is supported by 32 timber columns that, five centuries later, are every bit as sturdy and well preserved as when they were first installed. Chang Tomb is the first mausoleum to have been built, and it set the standard of design for the 12 other tombs that followed. ▼

Ding Tomb (Dingling)

Lying southwest of Chang Tomb below the Dayu Hill, Ding Tomb was built for Emperor Shenzong and his two queens. Started in 1584 when he was still alive, it was completed six years later. It features the Brilliant Tower, roofed with yellow-glazed cylindrical tiles and stone tablets inscribed with the words Da Ming (Great Ming) and Tomb of Shenzong, but otherwise there is little surface evidence of the far grander spectacle that lies under the ground behind this mausoleum entrance. ▼

The Underground Palace

Right behind the Brilliant Tower of Ding Tomb lies the Underground Palace, or burial tomb, of Emperor Shenzong and his two queens, the only burial hall excavated so far in the Ming Tombs. Archaeologists broke through to it in 1956 and found five chambers, each separated by a 4-ton stone door, that were as majestic as any of the Pharaonic tombs unearthed in Egypt.

Under the vast domed ceiling of the stone hall they found the coffins of Shenzong and his wives, along with golden crowns and other ceremonial headwear, porcelain, utensils, jade vases, silk wear and other burial possessions—the stone funerary bed lying in surroundings of bare simplicity compared with the decor and furnishings of the adjoining chambers. There, the floors are paved with "gold" tiles impregnated with tung oil to give them a lasting luster, and the central chamber features intricately carved white marble benches, blue porcelain urns with dragon motifs and other Ming dynasty artwork. ▲

QINGDONG MAUSOLEUMS
清東陵

The Qing dynasty buried its emperors on a series of sites, the earliest of them in the Qingdong Tombs in Zunhua County, 78 mi. (125 km) east of Beijing—a cluster of mausoleums that developed into the most extensive burial spot in China. The tombs were commenced in 1663, and emperors Shunzhi, Kangxi, Qianlong, Xianfeng and Tongzhi, along with their consorts and more than 100 concubines, were laid to rest. Though not as ornate as the preceding Ming dynasty tombs, these burial places followed basically the same pattern of Great Red Gate entrances opening on to sacred avenues—a 3.7-mi. (6-km) approach in this case—lined with stone sculptures of animals and statues of civil and military officers. ▲

YU MAUSOLEUM
裕陵

The largest of the Qingdong tombs is that of Emperor Shunzhi, but the most impressive are those of Qianlong (top opposite) and the empress Dowager Cixi. The interior walls of both tombs are richly carved and gilded, and the empress's resting place features many Buddha images, reflecting the devoutly religious side of her otherwise stubborn and imperious character.

QINGXI MAUSOLEUMS
清西陵

The other Qing dynasty monarchs were buried in the Qingxi Mausoleums, a resting place covering 598,000 sq. yd. (500,000 sq. m) in Yi County, Hebei. The whole mausoleum complex contains the tombs of four Qing emperors (Yongzheng, Jiaqing, Daoguang and Guangxu), three empresses, seven princes and a number of imperial concubines. The tombs here are more scattered than those at Qingdong Tombs but are considered architecturally more interesting and are set against a pleasant backdrop of wooded hills. ▶

Baotu Spring

趵突泉

Jinan City in Shandong Province is famous, among other things, for no less than 72 springs that gush up from a huge subterranean reservoir. The most celebrated of them is Baotu Spring, which has three "eyes" from which the water erupts in three fountains—a phenomenon that the famous calligrapher and painter, Zhao Mengfu of the Yuan dynasty, pictured as a white jade vase gushing out of the flat ground. The water is widely considered ideal for the making of tea, which by the Tang dynasty had become China's national beverage and such a ceremony and art that, simply to take a drink of it, the socially refined were advised to follow seven steps in the brewing and use 24 implements in the preparation and serving—and to forget it altogether if even one of these was missing. ▲

DAMING LAKE
大明湖

Lying north of Jinan, Daming Lake is a small body of water with a big history—a former pleasure spot for the educated classes of old Chinese society, and mentioned in a book written as far back as the 4th century. Its Lixia Pavilion, which stands on an island in the middle, was a favorite meeting place of the Tang dynasty poet Du Fu and Li Yong, the prefect of Beihai, and paintings of them are on display there. Around the lake there are other historic buildings, such as the a Yuan dynasty pavilion and a memorial temple to the Song dynasty governor of Jinan, the scholar Zeng Gong. ▼ ▶

THOUSAND BUDDHA HILL

千佛山

Remarkable Buddha images, carved into the rock (top, opposite), are a feature of Thousand Buddha Hill, just south of Jinan, the capital city of Shandong Province. The spot is also called Emperor Shun Farming Hill, because it was said that the legendary ruler, believed to have lived 4,000 to 5,000 years ago, grew the grain here with which he introduced his people to the principle of barter. A monastery, Xingguo (bottom, opposite), stands on the peak of the hill, with a gate marking its entrance.

Inscribed on it is a couplet that reads:

"The evening drums and morning bells shake up the people who hanker after profit and fame.
The sutra-chanting and Buddha prayers call back the people from the sea of bitterness and confusion."

The monastery's East Temple (Lishanyuan) was designed to embrace all three principal faiths, Buddhism, Taoism and Confucianism. ▼

Tai Mountain
泰山

Tai Mountain is another of the five most sacred mountains in China, associated with the father of Chinese social philosophy, Confucius, who was born in Shandong Province. For centuries—more than 40 of them—Chinese from the lowliest coolie to the emperors themselves have made pilgrimages to its 5069 ft. (1545 m) main peak. At the foot of the mountain is Taishan Temple, which was built in the Han reign and added to in the Tang and Song dynasties. Climbing the hill is no easy feat—a total of 7200 steps lead to the South Sky Gate, which opens on to the summit. From there, and its beautiful Jade Emperor Hall, visitors can enjoy four famous sights—The Sun Rising on Tai Mountain, Evening Colors, Golden Ribbon of the Yellow River and Sea of Clouds. ▲ ▶

Triumphal Gateway to Tai Mountain

A three-arched triumphal gateway (pailou) at the foot of Tai Mountain marks the spot where Confucius is said to have rested before making his own pilgrimage to the summit nearly 2500 years ago. On the peak, an outcrop of rock features inscriptions by other illustrious visitors, various emperors going back to the infatuated and ill-fated Xuanzong of the Tang dynasty. ◀ ▲

Black Dragon Pond (Heilongtan)

This body of water on the western approach to Tai Mountain creates a dramatic and picturesque waterfall, and a popular picnic spot, below the arch of the 75-ft. (23-m) single-span bridge. ▶

FOREST OF CONFUCIUS (KONGLIN)
孔林

This, probably the most significant historic site in China, is where Confucius and his descendants were buried. It lies about a mile (1.5 km) north of Qufu City in Shandong and boasts an ornate roofed gateway leading to the Forest of Confucius as well as a huge grove of 20,000 old and rare trees, some of which, it is claimed, were planted by Confucian disciples over the centuries. Aside from Confucian shrines and other buildings, the complex includes Xiang Hall, constructed in the Ming dynasty for sacrificial rites, and the tomb of a celebrated writer, Kong Shangren, who penned the drama *Peach-Blossom Fan*. ▼

THE CONFUCIUS GRAVE
孔子墓

After the death of Confucius in 479 BC, his disciples kept watch on his grave for three years. And according to the Shiji (Annals of History) by Sima Qian, one particular devotee, Zigong, carried on the vigil alone for another three years to demonstrate his love for the master and grief at his passing. To the west of the Confucius Grave in the Forest of Confucius, there is a terrace and three cottages bearing a tablet inscribed with the words "This is where Zigong kept watch." The grave itself has the burial spot of Confucius's son to its east and that of his grandson to the south, conforming to the traditional burial pattern of "carrying a son and grandson." A measure of the abiding devotion to Confucius is a 0.62-mi. (1-km) ceremonial avenue leading to the gravesite, flanked with all the imperial trappings of stone animal sculptures and statues of military heroes. ◀

CONFUCIUS RESIDENCE
孔府

Since Confucius set the ethical guidelines of Chinese society more than two millennia ago, successive dynasties have paid tribute to him and his descendants by bestowing honorary nobility on them and maintaining and expanding the master's residence. The present Confucius Residence, as it is called, was built in the Song dynasty between 1038 and 1039 and has burgeoned in the centuries since then to include 460 buildings, including halls, chambers and living quarters. All for the spirit of an ancient, albeit revered man. Each dynasty has also contributed some of the finest artworks of its period as furnishings and decoration, and Confucius Residence houses a priceless collection of porcelain and other ceramics, costumes, bronzes, weapons, furniture, screens, scrolls and calligraphy. ▼

CONFUCIAN TEMPLE
孔廟

Two years after Confucius died, the Prince of Lu ordered the construction of a temple on the original site of the great sage's house, declaring it a monument to the philosopher and a place of worship. Later, dynastic rulers added their own memorials, shrines and halls to the temple, eventually establishing a complex that covers an area of about 263,000 sq. yd. (220,000 sq. m) and is one of the most palatial sacred institutions in China. The temple's principal hall, Dacheng, houses a clay sculpture of Confucius, surrounded by images of his 12 closest followers and latter-day sages such as Yan Hui, Zeng Zi and Mencius. Inside another hall, Shengji, there are 120 engraved stone panels illustrating the great man's life. ▲

Apricot Terrace (Xing Tan)

Xing Tan (Apricot Terrace) is right in the middle of the passageway leading to the main hall called Dachengdian or Great Hall of Confucius. It is said to be the place where Confucius in his last years had delivered his lectures to his students.

Now it is a pavilion within the Confucian temple. Right next to the pavilion, there is an ancient Chinese juniper, believed to be planted by Confucius himself. The ornately painted pavilion with up-swept eaves has a double-tier roof covered with yellow glazed tiles. Inside the pavilion are elegantly carved stone columns sculptured with golden dragons, usually reserved only for the imperial families. There is also a stela endowed by emperor Qianlong of the Qing Dynasty with his Hymn to Xing Tan inscribed on it. The 3 ft. (1 m) high incense burner in front of the pavilion is a relic from the Jin dynasty. ▼

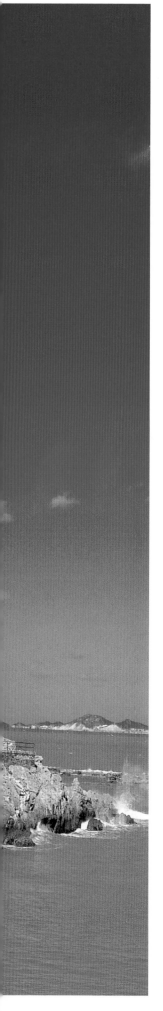

PENGLAI MANSIONS
蓬萊閣

The Eight Immortals, or Baxian, are legendary beings of the Taoist religion who are said to have achieved immortality through their discovery of the inner secrets of nature. They are also said to have the power of raising the dead, along with a "Midas touch" that will turn anything into gold.

Erected on the hills of Danya in Penglai County of Shandong, Penglai Mansions is a series of Taoist temples and monasteries said to be the Land of the Immortals. Perched above the Yellow Sea, usually enshrouded in mist, the mansions appear to be unreal. This is also the scene of an occasional optical illusion, something like a desert mirage, in which the landscape and landmarks of areas 62 mi. (100 km) away will appear over the waters. The mirages are frequent at the end of spring and at the beginning of the summer seasons and are particularly spectacular on a clear day following a rainstorm. In ancient times it was believed that these mirages spouted from the mouths of sea monsters. ◄

LAO MOUNTAIN
嶗山

Lao Mountain, a rocky mountain near the Shandong seaside resort and port of Qingdao, is another of China's sacred peaks. On its slopes there is a spring called Divine Spring, which, it is said, has never dried up, even in the most severe drought, and was regarded as the elusive and much coveted Elixir of Life by the ancients. Certainly, the first emperor of Qin, and Emperor Wu of the Han dynasty, are said to have visited Lao Mountain in search of the immortalizing potion. The mountain is also revered by Taoists as the home of many immortals. Among its temples and monasteries, the most sacred, is Taiqing Palace, first built in 140 BC during the reign of the Han emperor, Wu. ▼

THE YELLOW RIVER
黄河

The 3395-mi.- (5464-km-) long Yellow River is China's second largest river, winding through the provinces and autonomous zones of Qinghai, Sichuan, Gansu, Ningxia, Inner Mongolia, Shaanxi, Shanxi, Henan and Shandong before flowing into the Bo Sea. It has over 30 main tributaries and countless minor streams, covering an area of 289,575 sq. mi. (750,000 sq. km). It waters the vast loess tableland of Central China, picking up immense amounts of sand and mud that color its waters yellow and give it the highest volume of alluvial deposits of any river in the world.

This combination of enormous water volume and silt has, since time immemorial, made the Yellow River both benefactor and scourge of the millions of people living along its banks. In its lower reaches, near its estuary, it has often burst its banks or suddenly changed course altogether because of silt deposits, flooding large areas of land and killing many thousands of people. But it has also provided abundant water and fertile soil for agricultural settlement that may well have been the first to appear on earth.Peking Man has shown that human settlement had been established in the Yellow River Basin half a million years ago. At Banbo in Xi'an, excavation has unearthed a Neolithic village dating back some 6000 years, and Neolithic pottery, carved tortoise shells (used as writing

tablets in ancient times) and carved ox bones have been found in Henan Province. But an even more exciting find was made in 1963 when the fossilized remains of Lantian Man were unearthed in Shaanxi Province and proved to be a full 100,000 years older than Peking Man. Elsewhere in China, remains have been found of a proto-human or forerunner of man who existed 1.7 million years ago, and there is little doubt that these "ape men" also roamed the fertile and food-rich banks and alluvial plains of the Yellow River.

But that which the Yellow River has given humanity it has also, to a much lesser extent, taken away. Its terrible floods have given it the reputation of being "China's sorrow," wreaking untold disaster almost every year. According to records, over a period of 2000 years the river has flooded more than 1500 times, and there have been 26 occasions on which it has completely changed its course.

An indication of the violence with which it switched direction comes from records that show its course at one point in history as flowing around to the north of the Shandong Mountains, then into the Bo Sea, and at another point cutting south of them to join the Huai River and emptying into the Yellow Sea—the distance between the two estuaries being about 311 mi. (500 km).

Bayanhar Mountains

This confluence of three mountain ranges is the watershed between the Yellow and the Yangtze rivers. Bayanhar Mountains, a branch of the Kunlun Range, lie 19,685 ft. (6000 m) above sea level and are capped with snow most of the year. The northern slopes are easily accessible, while the southern slopes are full of ravines.

Despite their beauty—their Mongolian name means "the fertile mountains of dark green"—the upper slopes are cold, rocky and desolate with only sparse patches of grassland supporting a thin scattering of Tibetan nomads and their cattle and sheep. But when summer comes, the mountains' many glaciers and the lower melting snows send hundreds of streams into the muddy sweep of two of China's greatest rivers—the Yellow and Yangtze. ▼

First Bend of the Yellow River

Close to its source in Qinghai Province, the Yellow River takes shape as it emerges from the Gyaring Lake and becomes a river 164–197 ft. (50–60 m) wide and 3.3 ft. (1 m) deep—its waters so crystal clear that it resembles glass. It makes its first turn, called the Great Bend, in Maqu county, Gansu Province, before it flows around Jishi Mountains, regarded by the Tibetans as the "ancestor of the Yellow River." After passing this range, the river flows into Gansu and then turns on a wide loop back into Qinghai Province. Its waters then enter the loess region, and their pristine clarity turns to a silt-laden yellow murk. ▼

Upper Yellow River

The upriver section of the Yellow River begins at a place called Guide, where the waters crash down through two major gorges to flatten out in Xunhua, one of the 18 counties of Qinghai. For most of this stretch, the river is expansive and slow moving with a backdrop of craggy mountains. But beyond Xunhua it speeds up again into a rushing torrent, forced through some 19 gorges in Gansu Province and unnavigable for much of its flow. The majority of Qinghai's 5.4 million population live along the course of the Yellow River. ▶

Liujia Gorge

Liujia Gorge is probably the most spectacular spot along the upper course of the Yellow River. It is the point where the river takes a full 90-degree turn to the west on the border between Qinghai and Gansu provinces. The gorge can be reached by boat, and to many visitors the scene is reminiscent of the beautiful and strangely shaped outcrops of Guilin in the south. At this point on its course (see below), the river is already taking on its "yellow" hue, but the quantity of silt is only about 5 percent, even in flooding. Most of the silt is dumped into it by its tributaries, which in this area are the Tao, Datong and Huang Shui. ▼

Qingtong Gorge

When the Yellow River leaves the gorge region in Gansu and flows into Ningxia Huizu Autonomous Region, it is flanked on one side by the Tengger Desert and on the other by mountainous border areas. Qingtong Gorge lies in the middle of Ningxia, 4 mi. (6 km) long and cutting the Yinchuan Plain into north and south regions. It is a strategic area and was the site of many famous battles to protect the heartland of China, including those fought under General Ma Xian of the Han dynasty and the Tang general Li Jing. They were fierce and dangerous encounters, as described in an ancient poem.

> *"Soldiers sent to fight in Qingtong Gorge, Nine out of ten
> will never return."* ▲

Yellow River Bridge at Lanzhou

This is the first steel bridge on the Yellow River, built in 1907 by a German company, and it cost 306,000 taels of silver. It replaced a pontoon bridge that had served as a crossing since 1398 in the Ming period. According to the *Lanzhou Prefecture Gazette*, some 24 large boats were used as pontoons, and the whole structure was dismantled each winter when the waters froze over and horses and carriages could get across on the ice. ▲

183

Hukou Waterfalls

Subject of poetry, art and legend, Hukou Waterfalls is the second largest falls in China, located on the Yellow River. As the river winds like a yellow dragon through Central China, it narrows and plunges through a gap. This narrow space filled with the rushing river water suggests a teapot spout, which is the translation of the Chinese name for the falls. The yellow mists that rise high above the tumultuous water at the base of the falls have been called "smoke from the river" since on sunny days the yellow spray appears to turn gray and then blue, like smoke. The legendary hero Yu the Great of ancient China is said to have taken over the monumental task of controlling the flooding of the Yellow River from his father, who was killed for his arrogance at attempting to change this force of nature that is the Yellow River. Yu, instead, led the people to tunnel through mountains and cut through ridges to make a safe passage for the river. ◀

Three Gates Gorge (Sanmenxia)

When the Yellow River turns east near Tongguan, it enters the Yuxi ravine, in the middle of which lies Three Gates Gorge, one of the most dangerous parts of the waterway. Here, two rocky islands called God Gate (Shenmen) and Demon Gate (Guimen) stand in the middle of the river, cutting its waters into three channels. Of the three, the God Gate is deepest and Demon Gate most dangerous. In the Tang dynasty another waterway was cut north of the three channels to bypass the dangers of Three Gates Gorge, but the scheme failed: When the river was low, the channel was not navigable, and at high water it became as treacherous as the main flow. A path was eventually cut along the wall of a cliff to get around the torrent, and it can still be seen above Three Gates Gorge today. ▼

Yellow River at Mang Mountain

After Three Gates Gorge and some 80 mi. (130 km) of ravines, the Yellow River widens again as it flows past Mang Mountain, also called Bei Mang Mountain, which lies north of Luoyang and extends to Zhengzhou as part of the Qinling Range. The region is noted for its wealth of ancient tombs—a poem by Wang Jian of the Tang dynasty tells how "Mang Mountain has very little land to spare / It is cluttered up with old graves of Luoyang people." Another Tang dynasty writer, Zhang Ji, has put a more morbid air to it: "North of Luoyang lies the road to Mang Mountain," he wrote. "Funeral carts rattle their way in the autumn air."

From a high point on Mang Mountain, the river can be seen passing under two steel bridges. Terraced croplands along its banks testify that Mang Mountain is a place of life and industry as well as death. ▲

Down River

The Yellow River sweeps to the northeast after passing Kaifeng and Lankau counties and rushes over China's northern plains. It gets narrower and narrower until it reaches Dongping and Yanggu, where the river is only about a mile (1.5 km) wide. After traversing the North China Plain, the river joins the Dawen River and continues to flow northeast. Dongping features a lake that is the only natural lake on the river's lower reaches. After Changqing the river arrives in Jinan, capital of Shandong, the last great city in the Yellow River Basin, and from there it flows through a delta covering 927 sq mi. (2400 sq. km.) and into the Bo Sea. For all its majesty and intermittent wrath, the Yellow River flows through great distances of arid and semi-arid land and is affected by drought. The quantity of water that the river carries annually to the sea is 1695 billion cubic ft. (48 billion cubic m)—a mere one-twelfth the volume of the region's other great river, the Yangtze. ▶

HUANGLONG

The Central Region (South)

This region covers seven provinces, includes an immense basin that was once a lake, is linked by the main waters and tributary system of the nation's mightiest river—and, in many respects, can be called both the physical and emotional heartland of China. Its main artery is the Yangtze River, 3900 mi. (6300 km) long and the world's third biggest river after the Amazon and Nile. Its complicated spiderwork of waterways knits together a territory that encompasses the warm, temperate or semi-tropical provinces of Sichuan, Hubei, Hunan, Jiangxi, Anhui, Jiangsu and Zhejiang, all of which are rich agricultural areas producing most of the country's staple and "cash" crops, such as rice, cotton, silk, tobacco, peanuts, soybeans and the so-called "lusty leaf" tea, which in only three centuries or so has become the world's leading stimulative beverage.

With such an abundance of water—the Yangtze's network and most of China's 370 large lakes—the region also produces vast quantities of freshwater fish, and the Zhoushan Archipelago off Zhejiang Province reaches into China's richest offshore fishing ground. Just south of the Yangtze Delta, where the huge river meets the East China Sea, lies Shanghai, China's late-developing center of industry, finance and intellect and, with 17 million people, a metropolis now ranking in population with Greater Los Angeles.

Aside from the Yangtze, the region is dominated by the Sichuan Basin, once a mammoth prehistoric lake that was drained millions of years ago by the rise of the Earth's crust. High mountains surround this basin—the Qionglai Range to the west, Wu Mountains on the east, Daba Mountains to the North and to the south the Dalou Mountains, which form part of the Yunnan-Guizhou Plateau. In its northern reaches the basin rises to form the Chengdu Plain, named for its principal city, historic Chengdu, also called the "land of abundance." The eastern area of the basin is warm, wet and misty, with the city of Chongqing shrouded in fog for nearly 170 days each year. On the lower reaches of the Yangtze, the great river, in conjunction with the Han River, has transformed what was once a sprawling marshland into a lake district and a series of four plains in which the waters and the soil are so fertile that it is known as the "land of fish and rice."

The entire region is noted for its natural and in many areas, dramatic beauty, its landscape ranging from deep gorges carved through the hills by the Yangtze, "seas" of bamboo in the highlands around Sichuan, three famous sacred Buddhist mountains—Emei in Sichuan, Jiuhua in Anhui and Putuo in Zhejiang—the Province of a Thousand Lakes, Hubei, and the Huangshan (Yellow Mountain) in southern Anhui, which are renowned for their forests of pines, dramatic rock formations, "cloud seas" and hot springs.

As the heartland of China, this region has held the key throughout history to the domination of the entire empire. Its wealth was the ultimate target of constant tribal military pressure from the north. Since the Eastern Jin dynasty (AD 317-420), when the Chinese capital was moved to Nanjing, and when the later Song emperors were forced to move south, the region has been China's cultural center and most coveted economic prize—the scene of great battles and power struggles and famous cities that were first established and developed as long as 3000 years ago.

DADU RIVER
大渡河

The largest tributary of the Min River, the Dadu rises out of the Guoluo Moun-tains between Sichuan and Qinghai and compares with the Yangtze in its potential for hydroelectric power.

On its 559-mi. (900-km) course, its level falls no less than 9600 ft. (3000 m), and by the time it reaches the Min River at Leshan, its waters flow at a rapid speed. The world's largest stone Buddha image, which stands on the slope of Mount Lingyun overlooking the river, is believed to have been set up in the hope that its powers would tame the river's fury. ▽

DAO CHENG
稻城

Tucked away in the Qinghai-Tibetan Plateau region at 20,000 ft. (6300 m) above sea level is an area dotted with over 1100 lakes, framed by sacred snowcapped peaks that is home to thirteen monasteries. It rivals the fabled Shangri-La, the setting for the famous 1933 novel *Lost Horizons* by James Hilton. Its Tibetan name, Daoba, means "open land at the mouth of a valley," Daocheng is a truly hidden treasure, off the regular tourist route. Much of its 1200-sq. mi.-(3000-sq. km.-) area can only be reached on horseback. Of the many lakes, all glacier carved, the local population names Pearl Lake with its crystal-clear waters as the most beautiful. Part of the area contains the Yading Nature Reserve.

The two best known of the area's monasteries are Xiongden and Gongaling. The grand structure of Gongaling possesses an exquisite copper image of the bodhisattva Maitreya (the future Buddha) presented to the monastery by the Fifth Dalai Lama. Xionden Lamasery, on the other hand, houses tens of thousands of Buddhist scriptures and many figures of Buddha, including a sandalwood statue of Sakyamuni. It was built in 1415 at 13,468 ft. (4200 m) above sea level. ▲

FOUR SISTERS (SIGUNIANG SHAN)
四姑娘山

According to Tibetan legend, the four tallest peaks of the Qionglai Mountain Range in southwest China were once four sisters who fought bravely with a ferocious leopard to protect the treasured pandas of this beautiful mountainous region.

Located close to the Wolong Giant Panda Nature Reserve, a refuge for the giant panda, the lesser panda, the golden monkey plus many other animals, this mountainous region of China has been rightly called the Chinese Alps since it boasts the Fours Sisters, the highest of the peaks at 20,000 ft. (6250 m), and more than a hundred other peaks of 16,000 ft. (5000 m). Alpine lakes, dense hemlock forests, unspoiled wilderness and the drama of snowcapped peaks draw visitors to admire, hike, mountain-climb and study. The great differences between the high mountain ridges and the deep valleys were created long ago by folding and lifting of the Earth's crust; further work was done by glaciers that helped carve the steep mountain walls. The region's extreme weather changes are a product of competing influences: tropical monsoon and continental highland climates that make for a rich ecology, dramatic temperature difference between day and night and the perfect growing conditions for prized herbal medicines. ▶

JIUZHAIGOU (NINE VILLAGE VALLEY)
九寨沟

Surrounded by snowcapped mountains, this beauty spot in Jiuzhaigou County on the border of Sichuan and Gansu features dense forests, a total of 108 high-mountain lakes and one of China's most dramatic waterfalls. Its name refers to nine local villages, all inhabited by Tibetans. The lakes are so clear that on a fine, still day the rocky beds and underwater vegetation can clearly be seen—giving them the names Five-colored Lakes, Peacock Lake and Five-Flower Sea. It is regarded one of the best tour resorts in China. ▲ ▶

The Shuzheng Waterfall

Tumbling and dashing down a natural flight of stone steps, the Shuzheng Waterfall is about 200 ft. (62m) wide. It cascades some 50 ft. (15 m) down to one of the scores of terraced lakes below. Not surprisingly, the local Tibetans have given the falls and their surrounding wooded lakes the name "fairyland." ▲ ▶

Home of the Giant Panda

Jiuzhai Gully, abundant with bamboo, is also a main habitat of the giant panda, China's most unique and most endangered native animal and symbol of the World Wildlife Fund. In the summer the pandas move up into the cooler mountain areas, where Tibetan tribespeople operate ingenious bamboo watermills in a rustic form of hydroelectric power. In the winter, the "bear cats," as the Chinese call them, return to the valleys and are known to scavenge village gardens and rubbish dumps for food. ▶

YELLOW DRAGON MONASTERY (HUANGLONGSI)

黃龍寺

Close to the Jiuzhai Gully, in an area of "stair lakes" (tihu) at the foot of the snowcapped Xuebaoding, north of Songpan County in Sichuan, is Yellow Dragon Monastery, built in the Ming dynasty. The monastery was given its name, in turn, from a legend in which the Emperor Yu traveled the country some 4000 years ago attempting to find ways of controlling a great flood, and was aided by a yellow dragon. The lakes, which lie on different levels of the terraced slope, are formed by the waters of melting snows and are noted for the iridescence of their waters, caused by refracted sunlight (left).

The area is also noted for military expeditions that passed through its forests and lakes in legend and in recorded history. Some of the great generals of the Warring States (475–221 BC) are said to have marched their armies through the area, and it is recorded that the Tang dynasty general Huo camped there on a march north to suppress the Xiongnu and other nomad Tubo tribes. Not much is left of the Yellow Dragon Monastery—only a rear building—but a festival there each year attracts pilgrims from as far as the arid plains of Gansu and Qinghai. ▲

DUJIANG DAM
都江堰

This huge engineering project and its quaint ancient suspension bridge stand where a famous dam known as the "fish mouth" was built in the 3rd century BC to control the floodwaters of the Min River west of Guan County in Sichuan. Early records hailed the dam as a marvel, because "there is no fear of famine (in) this well-watered land." It removed the annual suffering from floods and helped turn Sichuan into one of the richest agricultural areas in China. ▲

TWO PRINCES TEMPLE
二王廟

Standing on the east bank of the Min River, this temple was originally built in tribute to a prince of the period of the Northern and Southern dynasties, which existed after the fall of the Han monarchs. But in ad 497 it was rededicated to Li Bing, the prefect of Shu County, and his son for building the vital Dujiang Dam. Its bamboo suspension bridge (replaced with steel cable now) has been known by several names over the centuries but is now popularly known as Husband-Wife Bridge, in honor of another family partnership responsible for its reconstruction in 1803. Each year thousands of people from all over Sichuan gather at the temple and slaughter sheep to celebrate the anniversary of the birthday of Li Bing's son. ▶

QINGCHENG MOUNTAIN
青城山

This mountain, with its 36 peaks and 72 caves, is typical of the quiet beauty of much of the Sichuan area and attracts many tourists. Lying southwest of Guan County, it features two sacred landmarks, the Tianshi and Shangqing temples. The Tianshi (Teacher from Heaven) Temple was built in the Sui dynasty, and its main hall houses a statue of Shen Nong, reputed to be the father of Chinese agriculture. Built in the Jin dynasty, the Shangqing Temple features a portrait of Laotze, who lived around 590 BC and founded Taoism, the native religion based on harmony between man and nature. Both temples were renovated in the late Qing dynasty. ▲

THE GREAT BUDDHA OF LESHAN
樂山大佛

Looming 233 ft. (71 m) high, with enough room on its crown to accommodate more than 100 people, this stone Buddha is the largest image in the world. In the Tang dynasty it was located in a thriving community of Buddhist monasteries, carved into the western wall of Mount Lingyun, southeast of Leshan in Sichuan Province. It took more than 90 years to construct and is believed to have begun in the year 713 by a monk who hoped to tame the sweeping currents of the confluence of three rivers— the Dadu, the Min and the Qingyi.

The Buddha was completed under the supervision of government officials in 803. It was once colorfully painted and gilded with gold leaf, and a 13-story pavilion, or Buddha House, protected it from the weather. The structure was destroyed in the late Ming dynasty, and the statue has been exposed—much to its cost—ever since. ▶

EMEI MOUNTAIN

峨眉山

The Song dynasty poet Fan Chengda wrote of Emei Mountain:

> "The Great Emei stretches its arms in friendly
>   welcome,
>
> While Little Emei and Middle Emei beckon in joy.
>
> Peerless they are in charm and elegance;
>
> No need to cross the seas for the Land of Immortals."

Soaring 10,171 ft. (3100 m) into the clouds in Emei County, Sichuan, this mountain was a sacred Taoist center as early as the East Han dynasty (ad 25–220), but its temples were taken over and rededicated in the spread of Buddhism. Since the Tang dynasty, it has been one of the four great Buddhist mountains of China. Several hundred monasteries were scattered around its lower slopes in its heyday, but now only a few remain, the most significant ones being Baoguo at the foot of the mountain, Wannian on its middle slope and Jinding at its summit. ◄

Wannian Monastery

East of the main peak of Emei Mountain, and below Double Dragon Mountain, only three of the original seven buildings of this Jin dynasty monastery still stand today. And those that are still there were renovated in the reign of the Ming ruler Wanli. The monastery possesses rare Buddhist sutras written on the leaves of the beiduoluo tree, as well as a 62-ton bronze sculpture of a Bodhisattva riding a six tusked elephant. ▼

DOUBLE DRAGON GORGE
雙龍峽

This gorge, along with its sisters—Dripping Green and Dragon Gate—is on the lower reaches of the Daning River, close to its meeting point with the Yangtze. The system of gorges is about 3 mi. (10 km) long, and its sides are so high in some places that low-lying clouds become trapped between the faces, creating an atmosphere of mystery and fantasy. Stalactite caves and strange rock formations enhance this atmosphere, conjuring up dramatic visions enriched by local lore. There is a winding ridge called the Dragon's Entry, and a cave characterized by a brown rock crossed with black veins called the Tiger's Exit, while four huge stalactites resembling two stallions burrowing their way head-first into the rock face are referred to as Horses Drilling through the Hills. ▷

DRIPPING GREEN (DICUI) GORGE
滴翠峽

This is one of the Daning River gorges, which is a 12-mi.- (20-km-) long stretch of sheer rock faces that tower about 1000 ft. (300 m) high and are known as Sky Scraping Red Cliff. There are, in fact, many other colors besides red in the rock—jade green, purple and blue, crimson and brown, silver, orange and yellow. The rock walls lie so close together, and the river's course bends at such acute angles, that there is another gorge, called Guanmenyan, or Closing Door Cliff, which appears to have no access at all until a boat virtually reaches its rock face. Then a narrow passage appears, only to "close" again when the boat is through. Around the gorge, lush vegetation has all but covered an ancient tribal stronghold called Luojiazhai, and there are weirdly shaped stalagmites and stalactites and a waterfall with such a fine curtain of spray that it is known as Flying Rain from the Heavenly Spring. ▲

DRAGON GATE GORGE
OF DANING RIVER
大寧河龍門峽

Called Wuxi in ancient times, the Daning River rises on a mountain slope on the border of Sichuan, Shaanxi and Hubei provinces and flows over 125 mi. (200 km) north to south to join the Yangtze at the entrance to Wu Gorge. The landscape through which it has carved its course is so precipitous and startling that it is called the Marvel of Gorge Country. As the river meanders south, it passes through seven dramatic gorges. The most renowned are the so-called Little Three Gorges comprising the Dragon Gate (Longmen), Double Dragon (Shuanglong) and Dripping Green (Dicui) gorges, stretching about 31 mi. (50 km) over the lower reaches of the river.

Longmen Gorge, also known as Luomen Gorge, is situated on the east of Wushan County. Going upstream from Wushan one would come to it before meeting the other two. The entrance to this mile- (3-km-) long gorge is guarded by two towering precipices like a gate, hence its name. ◄

STONE SCULPTURES AT DAZU
大足石刻

This horseshoe-shaped hillside tableau, northeast of Dazu County in Sichuan, was started in the Southern Song dynasty and took from 1133 to 1162 to complete. Later sculptures were added during the Ming and Qing reigns. Today, the statues, engravings and bas-relief images—more than 15,000 of them—rank with the grottoes at Mogao and Dunhuang in the legacy of early Chinese Buddhist art. Most of the sculptures refer to Buddhist stories and include the Six Paths of Reincarnation, Story of the Radiant Peacock Deity, Stories of the Allencompassing Buddha and the Transforming Phases of Hell. But the most dramatic and inspiring work by far is the huge recumbent Sakyamuni Buddha (above), which attracts thousands of Buddhist pilgrims each year.

These hill carvings, started in the late Tang dynasty and completed over a period of 250 years, cover no less than 45 sites in Dazu County. They were first commissioned by Weijing, the governor of Changzhou, around AD 892, and the work was carried on through the Five Dynasties and Northern Song periods and into the reign of the Song emperor Xiaozong. The Tang sculptures are among the finest, reflecting the sophistication and refinement of that age, and include Bodhisattvas with rosaries and upraised palms and accompanying dragons and other beasts, birds, landscapes, pavilions and mansions. It is ironic that, in an age in which Buddhist art achieved such distinction, the religion should have come under the hammer of imperial disapproval. However, when the relatively brief period of suppression ended, the invention of block printing enabled scholars to publish a vast bibliography of Buddhist translations, and the religion enjoyed new popularity and growth. ▲ ▶

LUGU LAKE
瀘沽湖

High in an isolated area of the province of Yunnan, Lake Lugu is home to one of the few existing matriarchal societies. The mountainous area of Lake Lugu has long been named the Female Kingdom by the Chinese. The remote land around the lake, located on a 900-ft.-(300-m-) high plateau ringed with towering mountains, has protected the culture of the matriarchal Mosuo people, who are part of the Naxi ethnic minority group. The pristine waters of Lake Lugu vary from intense blue and turquoise to milky gray-white. The lake is rich in carp and many other species of fish, and visitors will see a native-style fishing boat plying the waters.

An elaborate system of courtship, including an exchange of tokens, begins a relationship between Mosuo men and women, and when by mutual consent love and affection exist, there is often an agreement witnessed and celebrated by the families of the couple. But the word marriage does not define their relationship, called "axia"; instead the term "dear companion" serves the pair in this female-centered society. Men continue to live their entire lives at the home of their mother, visiting their "dear companion" each day. For the children of this relationship, the word father is not used. "Maternal uncle" defines this role in its place. Mosuo women are the leaders of the family, and goddess worship is practiced in this unusual mountain kingdom. ▲

Du Fu's Cottage
杜甫草堂

The bard Du Fu, who lived in the years AD 712-770 in the Tang dynasty, is regarded as one of the two greatest poets that China has ever produced. He was beloved for his sympathy for the poor and downtrodden victims of injustice and the almost constant casualties of Chinese history, those of internecine warfare. During the violent insurrection led by An Lushan against the hopelessly infatuated Emperor Xuanzong, Du Fu took refuge for four years in this small home on the western edge of Chengdu and managed to turn out about 240 poems. The cottage was rebuilt as a shrine in his name during the Northern Song dynasty, and its present design is the result of further renovation in the years 1500 and 1811. A statue of the great writer stands in an exhibition hall that was added to the home in the Qing dynasty. There is also a Qing tribute in the main study that reads:

"Let us contemplate the dearth of poets
of great stature through the centuries.
Here lived one whose cottage will last as
long as the land exists." ◄

Hall of the Three Sus
三蘇祠

This magnificent estate and residential complex in Sichuan's Meishan County stands on the site of the home of the celebrated Song dynasty literary family of Su Xun and his two sons, Su Shi and Su Zhe. Though all three men were noted bards and scholars, Su Shi (better known nowadays as Su Dongpo) became one of the dynasty's most famous poets—and governor of Hangzhou in 1089–1091—and there are memorials and tributes to him in various spots in Sichuan and Guangdong provinces. A memorial hall was added to the family estate in the Ming dynasty but was destroyed. It was rebuilt in 1665 and redeveloped in 1928 and named the Three Sus' Park. The Great Hall (Qixian) features some of the literary works of Su Shi and his relatives, along with stela rubbings of their calligraphy, while the corridor built above the pond divides the waters into two parts. ▶

ZHANGJIAJIE

張家界

Zhangjiajie may refer to the city that used to be called Dayong, as well as the Zhangjiajie National Forest Park, the first national park in China established in 1982. It is one of the four scenic spots of a greater scenic area called Wulingyuan, the other three being Yangjiajie, Suoxiyu and Tianzi Mountain, covering a total area of close to 300 sq. mi. (500 sq. km). Formerly known as Green Cliff Mountain, noted for its picturesque or bizarre rock formations, Zhangjiajie is a group of 2000 mountain peaks at the junction of three counties in Hunan Province. Legend and imagination have given the peaks various names, such as Golden Whip Boulder, in memory of an incident in which the first emperor of Qin is said to have lost a whip there. Other peaks are known as Three Sisters, Rooster Cliff, or Monkeys-Storming-Heavenly-Palace Peak, depending on their shapes. ◄ ▲

FENGHUANG CITY

鳳凰城

In Western Hunan, the small town called Fenghuang—or Phoenix City in Chinese—is a wonderful place to see the Miao, one of China's best-known ethnic minorities. Legend, history, Miao architecture and customs are all part of a visit. There are two very different stories for the name of the town. Legend has it that a pair of phoenixes were once spotted in the area, but, once noticed, they flew away. A more historical account ignores the idea of the mythical birds altogether and tells of the town growing from a Han military camp situated there to quell the rioting Miao. Many of the soldiers stayed, and now the town is inhabited by both the Miao and the Han Chinese. One of China's great 20th century writers grew up in Phoenix City, where his father was in the military. This author, Shen Congwen, wrote many novels, and one of his most popular presents a vivid picture of the Miao life, when the natives still wear ethnic costume and preserve the Miao folk songs. Visitors can take a ride in the slim wooden boats of the Miao. The enticing smell of ginger candy wafts into the streets from the many candy workshops. Once a year, during the time the rest of China celebrates the Dragonboat Festival, the local people have their own wild and exciting day, called Duck Chasing. Thousands of ducks specially gathered for this amazing free-for-all are released into the river. A gripping chase follows, and whoever catches the ducks keeps them!

The peculiar Miao building style called hanging attic is used in houses that line the riverbank. Although the foundations look precarious, the houses using traditional methods are safe, sturdy homes and have sheltered the Miao for many decades. ▲

Qu Yuan Temple
屈子祠

This imposing temple, with its red-pillar facade, was erected in memory of Qu Yuan, who in 278 BC threw himself into the Miluo River in grief at the defeat of his state of Chu in the Warring States struggle. At the rear is a mound where he is believed to have written his famous *Li Sao* (The Sorrow of Parting). His suicide has since been commemorated by the annual Dragon Boat Festival. During the boat races people throw rice into the waters, re-enacting a gesture in which rice and other food were thrown where he drowned to keep fish and turtles away from his body. ▶

Lake Dongting
洞庭湖

Lying in the northern reaches of Hunan Province and covering an area of 1081 sq. mi. (2800 sq. km), Lake Dongting is the second biggest freshwater lake in China. Its name means Cave Home of Immortals, and therefore it has always been a sacred spot. Its nearby Jun Hill, one of the few islands on the lake, was once packed with 48 temples and 36 pavilions, but most of them were destroyed over the centuries by fire or civil strife. Only a handful remain, including Two Concubines Tomb, and Wine Fragrance Pavilion. The lake has 11 towns dotted around it in an area that produces cereals, fish, lotus products and tea. Another noted product is two rare species of bamboo: Xiang Concubine, named after the two concubines buried there, and Luohan. ▲

YUEYANG MANSION

岳陽樓

This majestic building stands at the western gate of Yueyang City in Hunan on a site that has a history going back to the Han dynasty. It is said that in the period of the Three Kingdoms, which followed the Han rule, one of the warring generals, Lu Su, used it as his command post. The mansion itself was first built by Zhang Shuo in the Tang dynasty, and it became an inspiration for several noted poets. In the Song period the mansion was renovated and the poet Fan Zhongyan was invited to write about it. He came up with his celebrated "Yueyanglouji." The keynote was depicted in these somewhat existentialist lines:

"To feel concerned before the world feels concerned;
To enjoy only after the world has started enjoying."

The present mansion is the result of another extensive renovation in 1880, and the building—along with its splendid tilework—has since been compared with the famous and recently restored Yellow Crane Mansion of Wuchang, and Tengwang Mansion in Nanchang. ▲

HENG MOUNTAIN
衡山

Known as South Sacred Mountain in ancient times, Heng Mountain and its 72 peaks run for a distance of over a hundred miles through the middle of Hunan Province. Its tallest peak, Zhurong, at 4232 ft. (1290 m) above sea level, is a favorite spot for viewing the sunrise. Naturally, it has also been a favorite haunt of poets, including the Song dynasty bard Huang Tingjian who, standing on Zhurong's summit, saw "Looking up, the myriad stars I strain to touch/Looking down, the dusty world is far, far away." ▲

Nanyue Great Temple

This palatial Great Temple of South Sacred Mountain stands on a site first developed in the Tang dynasty in Nanyue Town at the foot of Hunan's Heng Mountain. Its main hall was rebuilt in 1882. It consists of nine main buildings, including two halls, pavilions, a library and the imposing Kuixing Mansion; the structure of the main hall includes 72 pillars representing the 72 peaks of the southern range. A circular stone balustrade around the hall is decorated with 144 marble panels carved with landscapes, birds, beasts, flowers and insects. Much of the complex is in the architectural styles of the Song and Ming dynasties, reflecting the renovation and extensions that have taken place since the Tang reign. A large iron bell was installed in the temple in the Yuan period, and the poet Li Bai wrote a tribute to Heng Mountain that was inscribed in the later age of the Ming on a stela and can be studied there today. ▲

WUDANG MOUNTAIN
武當山

Otherwise known as Taihe Mountain, Wudang includes 72 peaks and 36 cliffs and covers an area of 155 sq. mi. (400 sq. km) in Jun County, Hubei. It also has so many scenic spots—caves, springs, pools, terraces and fountains—that Mi Fu, the great calligrapher of the Song dynasty, gave it the reputation, still alive today, of being the Prime Mountain of China. The mountain is a sacred place in Taoism, the religion based on harmony with nature, and many Taoist disciples in ancient times came here to perfect their disciplines, including Zhang Sanfeng of the Ming period, who introduced a style of martial art called Wudang boxing. In the Ming dynasty, as many as 300,000 people were recruited to build a Taoist monastery here that included 72 cliff temples. ▼

Zixiao Temple

Built in the Yuan dynasty in 1413, this temple northeast of Wudang Mountain's Sky Pillar Peak has a main hall featuring an august and dignified statue of the Jade Emperor, the supreme master of the Taoist gods. Also known as the Pearly Emperor, Yu Huang, the Jade Ruler is one of three supreme deities—the Pure Ones—of Taoism. It is believed that he was borrowed from the Buddhist hierarchy, the Buddhists adapting him in turn from Brahma, the almighty creator of Hinduism. He stands majestically in the Zixiao Temple's principal hall surrounded by statues of his attendant gods. This temple is one of the finest on Wudang Mountain and is designed to harmonize so ingeniously with the craggy terrain that its buildings create a novel "exposing and hiding" effect in which some seem to appear while others disappear as visitors walk along a mountain path leading to the complex. Other buildings in the temple are the Dragon and Tiger Hall (Longhudian), containing sculptures of both beasts, and a stela pavilion featuring two 10-ft. (3-m) high stone sculptures of tortoises. ▲

Bronze Statue of Zhenwu

The regal, corpulent 10-ton statue of Zhenwu rests in the Golden Hall of Wudang Mountain in the province of Hubei. It is flanked with statues of the traditional servants, Golden Boy and Jade Girl, and attended by two bodyguards, the Fire General and Water General, both in the act of drawing their swords. Built in 1416, the Golden Hall lies on the summit of Wudang's Sky Pillar Hill. ▼

SHENNONGJIA
神農架

Originally the site of an old glacier, this mountain range overlooks the Yangtze River between Hubei, Shaanxi and Sichuan provinces and covers an area of 1236 sq. mi. (3200 sq. km). The highest peak, rising to over 9800 ft. (3000 m), is called the Roof of Central China. The name Shennongjia is derived from the story of Shennong, mythical father of herbal medicine who "tasted the myriad herbs" for their medicinal qualities. Shennong is believed to have built a lodge on this mountain range, distilled the Elixir of Life there, and then turned into an immortal—whereupon the lodge became a forest. The region is in fact rich in plant life. More than 2000 species grow on the slopes, including rare medicinal herbs such as ginseng, angelica sinensis, gastrodia elata and eucommia. A habitat for over 500 species of wildlife, it is the home of bears, South China tigers, "gold coin" leopards, deer, flying squirrels, wolves, pandas and monkeys. In recent years strange unidentified five-toed footprints one and a half feet (half a meter) long have been sighted—so far the largest footprints in the world to be recorded. ◀

Swallows Pass (Yanziya)

This high mountain pass 22 mi. (35 km) northeast of Shennongjia is almost constantly enveloped in clouds and mist, so much so that it is known as the mountain that "never sees summer." It is also constantly raining there, so the vegetation is naturally lush. The mountain wall also features a huge cavern called Swallows Cave, which includes an opening section big enough for a thousand people to gather in and an inner sanctum in which thousands of swallows nest all year-round. A rare bird called wogehui ("My brother, come back") inhabits the slopes, named after a legend in which a maiden mourned the loss of her brother so bitterly that she transformed into a bird of that name. ▲

GREEN SHADOW WALL
(LUYINGBI)
綠影壁

B uilt over 500 years ago, this Green Shadow Wall of alum shale bricks is typical of Taoist shadow walls built throughout China before the gates of official buildings to deflect evil spirits and other "noxious influences." Sometimes an enormous red sun was depicted on the walls to reflect the pure and bright principle of yang and to encourage civil servants to observe diligence and justice. The Luyingbi stands at the gate of a palatial Ming dynasty mansion complex in Xiangyang City in Hubei. In 1858, it was destroyed in the Taiping Rebellion, but the wall survived. Ninety-nine dragons are carved on the wall, and once they played with a pearl "bright as the sun," referring to the legend of what is believed to have been a solar eclipse in Xiangyang. The pearl is now missing. ▲

GUQIN TERRACE
古琴台

T his beautiful terrace and hall, enclosed in a white marble balustrade, lies beside the Moon Lake in Hanyang, Hubei. Its name means Ancient Zither Terrace, and it was first built in the Northern Song dynasty nearly 1000 years ago to commemorate the deep friendship of a qin (zither) master, Yu Boya, and a recluse named Zhong Ziqi of the Spring and Autumn Period of 770–476 BC. Their love and understanding of each other and music was so strong that when Zhong died, the zither maestro destroyed his instrument, vowing never to play again. The term zhiyin (music understood) has since been synonymous with true friendship. ▲

SITE OF THE MILITARY REGIME
軍政府舊地

A bronze statue of Dr. Sun Yatsen, the founder of the 1911 Chinese republic that replaced some 3000 years of dynastic rule, stands at the gate of this former government headquarters in Wuchang, Hubei Province. Before the republican revolution the buildings and their central watchtower were used as a training base for the Qing imperial cavalry. When the Qing dynasty was toppled in 1911, it became the temporary headquarters of the republican provisional government. Now it has become a museum commemorating that revolution. ▲

EAST LAKE
東湖

Covering 13 sq. mi. (33 sq. km), East Lake lies to the east of Wuchang and has so many inlets and curves around its bank that it is also known as the "lake with no limit." It is surrounded by six scenic and historic spots that are called Tingtao (Listening to the Waves), Mo (Mill) Hill, Luoyan (Descending Wild Duck), Baima (White Horse), Chuidi (Playing the Pipe) and Luohong (Gem). The Tingtao section features an island and a three-story mansion called Hangyinge (Strolling Chanting Mansion) with a statue of the poet Qu Yuan—its name referring to a line in his epic *Sorrow of Parting* that tells of "strolling by the marsh, chanting." Nearby is the Nine Women Pier commemorating women martyrs who died in battle against the Manchu Qing forces in the 1858 Taiping Rebellion. Other spots feature monasteries and monuments going back to the Tang and Song dynasties, and even further back to the time of the state of Wu. ▲

GULONGZHONG
古隆中

This is the place where the strategy of a divided China, separating the country into three distinct states, was formulated prior to the Three Kingdoms Period of AD 220–280. It was also where Zhuge Liang, the brilliant political and military tactician of the state of Shu, is said to have spent 10 years as a recluse in a cottage before being persuaded to serve as prime minister to the Prince of Shu. ▼

YELLOW CRANE MANSION
黃鶴樓

Yellow Crane Mansion is one of three famous towers south of the Yangtze River that have been celebrated in Chinese verse for centuries. Also called Huanghe Lou, this mansion is the chief landmark of the port city of Wuchang. Located in Hubei Province, its superb view of the Yangtze River has been acclaimed through the ages. Built in the year 233 AD, it was long a magnet for artists and writers to gather nearby, drink wine and write poetry, a favorite literary pastime. A legend tells that the name of the tower comes from a magic crane drawn on the wall of a local wine shop by a visiting Taoist priest in thanks for the owner's free wine for the thirsty visitor. The painting was magic because the crane would dance when someone clapped his hands. This magic wall painting brought much business and great success to the shopowner. A decade after the crane was painted, the legend goes, the priest returned to the wine shop, played his flute, jumped on the crane's back and then disappeared into the sky.

Time had ravaged the ancient tower, but it was reconstructed on the original site after a four-year restoration in 1985. A visit today illustrates why the mansion and its view is still a place for inspiration and a subject of more than 300 poems in the long history of Chinese literature.

▼

GANTANG LAKE
甘棠湖

Fed by streams from Lu Mountain, this lake in the center of Jiujiang City was originally called South Gate Lake and features a long dike with an elegant balustrade built in the Tang dynasty. It leads to the Yanshui Pavilion, originally erected in the time of the Tang. From here, visitors can climb to a panoramic viewpoint at Yingyue Mansion. Elsewhere the lake features an old monastery and pagoda, along with the Suojiang (Lock River) Mansion and Langjing (Wave Well), whose name comes from the saying: "When the Yangtze River heaves with waves, even the wells respond with ripples." ▲

Yanshui Pavilion

Standing in the middle of Gantang Lake in Jiujiang City, Jiangxi, this pavilion is relatively new—built with funds raised by a monk named Gu Huai in the latter part of the Qing dynasty. But the history of the site is considerable. It goes back to the raising of an army in the Three Kingdoms Period more than 1700 years ago, and it is where two pavil-

ions were built in the Tang dynasty and the reign of the Northern Song, only to be demolished in 1522. In the Ming reign another pavilion was erected there, but it eventually met the same fate—pulled down in 1853. ▲

Lu Mountain
盧山

This, one of China's most delightful mountains, rears to the south of Jiujiang City and overlooks the Yangtze River. Its name Lu means lodge, and legend says it was where seven brothers named Kuang built a lodge in the time of the Zhou dynasty (1050–221 BC). Legend also has it that the great healer, Dong Feng, one of the noted mountain shamans of early Chinese history, made his home at the foot of the mountain. He is said to have refused payment for his services and usually asked his patients to plant five apricot trees when they recovered. In the time of the Eastern Han dynasty (AD 25–220) more than 380 monasteries existed on the mountain's slopes, a few of which still stand after centuries of care and renovation. Lu Mountain's "sea of clouds" is a celebrated tourist attraction, as are its many peaks, caves, pools and waterfalls. ◄ ▼ ►

WUYUAN
婺源

ituated northeast of Jiangxi Province near the borders of Anhui and Zhejiang, Wuyuan County is endowed with that special beauty so admired in Chinese landscape painting. Its rolling mountains, crystal-clear creeks, bamboo forests, strange rock formations, caves, tea plantations and ancient trees are the perfect inspiration for the painter and poet, and yet it has been largely overshadowed as a destination by the nearby Yellow and Lu mountains. The other attraction in the area for visitors from all over the world is the famous porcelain capital Jingdezhen.

Wuyuan, with its idyllic scenery, has in fact long been a favorite for poets and writers over the ages, but because of its seclusion it has remained a hidden secret until recently when vacationers, tired of the usual tourist destinations, began to look for new places with historical interest as well as natural beauty. Visitors are entranced by Wuyuan County's villages and countryside, claimed to be the finest in China.

As for history, Wuyuan County boasts some of the best preserved ancient architecture from the Ming and Qing dynasties. It even boasts an 800-year-old covered Rainbow Bridge (below) of the Song dynasty. Scholarship has had a long tradition also. Wuyuan has produced an amazing number of scholars who passed the imperial court exams, 550 in all. Probably the best known is Zhu Xi, a late Song dynasty scholar, who was the co-founder for the Cheng-Zhu Confucian School and who wrote what was later accepted as the standard interpretation of Confucian learning in the imperial examinations.

In ancient times Wuyuan was counted as part of Anhui's Huizhou Prefecture and was known for being the home of one of the three most influential merchant groups in China, called the Hui merchants. Finally, green tea from Wuyuan is well known in China and is one of the few teas that have passed the rigorous organic certification tests of the European Union in 1997. ▼

PRINCE TENG (TENGWANG) MANSION

滕王閣

For generations, the fame of Prince Teng Mansion is due to the widely read poem titled *Preface to Tengwang Mansion*, written over a thousand years ago by one of the four popular early Tang dynasty poets, Wangbo. The best-known lines are: "A solitary bird glides in the sunset glow / The autumn waters mingle with the hue of the sky." In the long tradition of the literary arts in China, later poets and scholars added further to the reputation of Teng Mansion by composing poems and prose extolling the view from the tower. Located on the bank of the Gan River, west of Nanchang City, Prince Teng Mansion is the most widely known of the three famous mansions south of the Yangtze river. The other two, Yueyang Mansion and Yellow Crane Mansion, are featured elsewhere in this book.

First built in AD 653 by Prince Li Yuanming, a younger brother of Emperor Taizong of the Tang dynasty, while he was governor of Nanchang, it was destroyed and rebuilt as many as 28 times until it finally burned to ashes in 1926. The current nine-storied Tengwang Mansion structure stands 190 ft. (58 m) high and was built in 1989 in the architectural style of the Song dynasty, with overhanging eaves that curve upwards at the corners and engraved beams. This newest reincarnation of this ancient building has beautifully restored the fabled grandeur of this 1300-year-old mansion. ▲

Judge Bao Temple
包公祠

Judge Bao, also known as Xi Ren, lived in the Northern Song reign and was noted for his incorruptibility and steadfast refusal to bend to official pressure. People called him Bao Qingtian (Bao Blue Sky) because of the clear, unclouded quality of his character. The temple in his name was built in the Ming dynasty on a small island in the River Bao in Hefei County, Anhui. It features, among other things, a well called Incorruptible Fountain, whose waters are said to give any blemished drinker a telltale headache.

▶

Taibai Mansion
太白樓

This three-story mansion, with its flamboyant flying eaves, was first built between AD 806 and 820 in memory of one of the greatest poets of China, Li Bai (701–762). Aside from his works, Li Bai is renowned for having tried to "catch the moon" (or its reflection) in a river after a number of drinks and almost drowning. The mansion stands in Caishiji, southeast of Ma'anshan County in Anhui, and its present design follows renovation that was carried out at the end of the 19th century. A large screen facing the main gate bears a painting of Li Bai on a visit to Caishiji, and in the shrine itself there are two wooden sculptures of the famous bard. ▼

Home of Badashanren
八大山人故居

This splendid white-walled former monastery in Nanchang, Jiangxi Province, was taken over in 1661 by the painter Chu Da, better known as Badashanren, a descendant of Ming royalty who sought refuge from the newly installed Manchu Qings. Called upon to serve his new masters, he feigned madness. He also kept himself inebriated to avoid being done away with under suspicion of conspiring against his Qing masters. For all that, Chu Da managed to continue painting and is highly regarded for the economy of his brushstrokes in ink painting. His influence on Chinese art has been considerable, and his style is much admired and imitated by traditional artists even today. ▶

Jiaonu Terrace
教弩台

Aside from including one of the most beautiful and best-preserved monasteries in Anhui Province, Jiaonu Terrace has a history that goes back to the East Han dynasty of AD 25–220. It is said that Chief Minister Cao Cao built Jiaonu Terrace as a training ground for a force of 500 archers to prepare for an attack by one of his two main rivals, Sun Quan, the warlord of the state of Wu in southeast China.

The monastery that stands on the terrace was originally called Iron Buddha Monastery. First built in the 5th centu-ry, it was renamed Ming Jiao Yuan and then Ming Jiao Si. There is a 20-ft. (6-m) high iron Buddha weighing 6 tons in the monastery. The monastery was rebuilt in 1870, and a new Da Xiong Bao Dian (Hall) was built in 1886. The main entrance has steps leading to the terrace. A gate stands there with a single-eave half-hipped, half-gabled roof. The Da Xiong Bao Dian itself is double-eaved with a half-hipped, half-gabled roof, covered with cylindrical tiles and devoid of brackets. The monastery is well shaded and possesses many stone sculptures. ▲

NINE FLOWERS MOUNTAIN (JIUHUA SHAN)
九華山

Lying in Qingyang County of Anhui, this craggy mountain area took its name from a poem by the Tang dynasty bard Li Bai. It has also been recognized for centuries as the Citadel of the Buddhist Empire. As long ago as AD 401, a Buddhist monk built himself a meditation retreat here, and at the advent of the Tang dynasty the king of Xinluo began erecting other places of worship. During the Song and Ming dynasties, and into the Qing reign, so many institutions were added that at one point the hills contained more than 400 monasteries for more than 4000 monks and nuns. Just over 70 of those places have survived, along with a rich legacy of about 1500 Buddha images and valuable paintings and murals and ancient sutra prints. The mountain range covers 39 sq. mi. (100 sq. km) and includes 99 peaks, the tallest, Shiwang (top), rising to 4403 ft. (1342 m). ▲

Tiantai Temple

On the summit of Sky Terrace Peak on Jiuhua Mountain is a beautiful temple first built in the Ming dynasty. It is called Tiantai Temple, also called the Ksitgarbha Temple. Wood columns and beams are the framework for the group of three five-story buildings with roofs of small black tile. The temple houses a great number of Buddhist statues and wooden sculptures. One of the most unusual aspects of this mountain monastery is found on the path leading to Sky Peak Terrace: the huge footprint said to have been left by Ksitigarbha. ◀

Gubaijing Terrace

This Tang dynasty monastery, rebuilt in the reign of the Qing emperors, perches on a terrace under the sheer face of Jiuhua's Tiantai Peak and is said to have been the place where Bodhisattva Kitigarba paid homage to the sutra in the year AD 653. An engraved footprint of the distinguished visitor is still on display there. This patron saint of Jiuhua is worshipped as a ruler of the Buddhist nether world, and his task is to free suffering souls from purgatory. He is also protector of infants. ▲

Qiyuan Monastery

The monastery took its name from the garden where Sakyamuni resided when he lived in this world. One of the four great surviving monasteries of Jiuhua Mountain, this building very nearly crumbled into ruin within years of its construction some time after 1522 in the Ming reign. With no resident abbot to maintain it, the monastery was in a state of disrepair when the Zen master Longshan stepped in and saved it. It soon became a flourishing Zen center, attracting great numbers of worshippers each year, and when Longshan died, it passed into the hands of two of his disciples. The monastery has an unusual asymmetrical layout. Its principal architectural feature is the striking gold glazed tiles. The front hall features a carving of a three-eyed god brandishing a whip and an inscription that warns:

"With three eyes to oversee the world's affairs,
With a lash to give warning to all people."

Inside the rear hall, there are three gilded Buddhas, each about 20-ft. (6-m) tall. These are the largest Buddha images in the Jiuhua Range. They are flanked by the 18 arhats, each sculpted with a different facial expression. The walls behind these images are decorated with colorful murals depicting stories from the Buddhist scriptures, adding solemnity to the decor of this big hall. ▼

TIANZHU MOUNTAIN
天柱山

Scenes of arresting grandeur greet the eye from all directions on top of the highest rocky terrace of Tianzhu Mountain after a 1700-step climb up the Sky Stairs. Standing at about 4882 ft. (1488 m), the main peak of Tianzhu Mountain is a huge granite rock about 656 ft. (200 m) high, which juts straight into the sky. Intrepid hikers on the way to the summit will find carved on the surface of the mountain's rock eight characters: "a solitary pillar that props up the sky," put there by an herb collector named He with the help of a couple of stonemasons in 1861. Later in 1944, the herb collector's great-grandson went up and carved four more characters, meaning "a solitary pillar in the sky."

Strange rock formations are a major attraction of Tianzhu, along with numerous caves, some of which hold tens of thousands of people. It is also full of cultural and religious relics. Identified as the sacred southern mountain during Han dynasty, Tianzhu has over the ages drawn many poets, scholar, Taoist and Buddhist monks there to establish temples and academies. While many of these are gone today, the restored Sanzu Temple and the stone carvings remain. A typical place to see the stone carvings is the Rock Cattle Creek in the Culture Valley, where more than 280 stone carvings can be found along a 656-ft. (200-m) long stretch of the creek, claimed to be an open "cultural museum of literature and arts." ▲

Hong Village and Xidi Village in Anhui Province

宏村和西遞村

In the year 2000, two well-preserved villages in the southeast of Anhui Province were listed as World Cultural Heritage sites. These beautiful villages, with many houses built 300–400 years ago, are tucked in a green, hilly area of Anhui. Xidi and Hong villages have long been admired by visitors and scholars of Chinese domestic architecture, but it was not until the year 2000 that any of China's ancient houses have been put on this prestigious worldwide preservation list. Xidi Village has the oldest houses, some dating back more than 400 years. An astounding number of houses, 122 in all, share elaborately shaped eaves and courtyards paved with dark-grey flagstones or closely spaced pebbles in traditional designs. Seen from above, this small village of tightly spaced houses resembles a ship sailing the green hills of the area.

Hong villagers, on the other hand, claim that their village is as strong as an ox. A hike into the surrounding hills to view Hong Village from above reveals the resemblance to an ox resting on its side by a river after hard labor. The Chinese delight in finding resemblances to nature in their man-made creations, and in this lovely example the Hong Village entrance is the ox's head, and the trees there have been called the horns of the ox's head. The comparisons to an ox continue and include the bridges like hooves, and

the body being the hundreds of closely spaced houses. The water around the village also fits the picture, with the river flowing alongside the village being the ox tail; a pond shaped like the stomach, and the intestines the network of the ditches essential to supply fresh water to every household. ▲ ▼ ▶

YELLOW MOUNTAIN (HUANG SHAN)

黄山

Legend has it that the Yellow Emperor once tried to distil the Elixir of Life on this magnificent mountain between She and Taiping counties in Anhui. A Pailou (entrance arch) announces the area, the beauty of which has been celebrated for centuries. The great Ming dynasty traveler Xu Xiake paid it the warmest of all tributes when he wrote: "Having returned from the Five Sacred Mountains, one does not want to look at ordinary mountains; having returned from Yellow Mountain, one does not want to look at the Five Sacred Mountains."

Yellow Mountain's main peaks all rise over 5900 ft. (1800 m), and the area is noted for its forests of pines, two lakes, three waterfalls, 24 streams, 72 peaks, its hot springs and its "sea of clouds."

The sheer-cliffed peak, on which stands a solitary rock called Feilaishi or Flown Here Rock (opposite, top) is one of the favorite places with a panoramic view of the scenic area. ▼ ▶

Yuping Peak

Rearing in petrified waves towards the sky, Yuping (Jade Screen) Peak is another dramatic aspect of the Yellow Mountain area. It looms between Lian-hua (Lotus Blossom) and Tiandu (Heavenly Capital) peaks and is close to the range's hot springs. It also features the Yuping Lodge, a well-positioned resting place for the weary climbers, which is said to stand where a monk, Pumen, dreamed of the Bodhisattva Manjusri in the year 1614 and erected a shrine to commemorate the vision. At 5512 ft. (1680 m), the entire peak is granite and was obviously created by some cataclysmic eruption hundreds of millions of years ago. This explains why both the ascent and descent are treacherous. Ways are steep, and one of the most dangerous points is the Xiao Xin Po (Be Careful Slope), which has a sheer wall on one side and overlooks a deep ravine on the other. Nearby lies the pretty, high-altitude Yuping Sky Lake. ▼

ZHONGSHAN MAUSOLEUM
中山陵

This, the mausoleum of Sun Yatsen, the father of republican China, was built between 1926 and 1929 on the southern slope of Mao Mountain, east of Nanjing in Jiangsu Province. Facing south, the layout follows that of traditional Chinese tombs, a sacred arch and avenue (this one stepped) leading to a main gate, stela pavilion, podium, tomb hall and then the grave chamber. The entire mausoleum is set in some 861,140 sq. ft. (80,000 sq. m) of forest and gardens. Dr. Sun Yatsen was born in 1866 in Guangdong Province and for years was an activist seeking to reform or overthrow the hidebound Manchu Qing dynasty—but, like Russia's Lenin, was forced to spend much of his time outside China in England, the U.S., Europe and Japan. He returned from exile in 1911 to claim victory and set up a provisional republican government after a successful uprising by urban workers supported by dissident units of the Qing army. ▼

PRESIDENTIAL RESIDENCE IN NANJING

南京總統府

The former presidential residence of the Kuomintang Party in Nanjing has been turned into a contemporary Chinese history museum, which has been expanded to its original size.

The western garden houses the office of Dr. Sun Yat-sen, China's first democratically elected president. Visitors may also see exhibitions of historical materials from the office of the Jiangsu governor of the Qing dynasty (1644–1911) and the palace of the Taiping Heavenly Kingdom (1851–64), pictures and documentation about Dr. Sun Yat-sen and historical materials belonging to the former presidential office.

Some experts have pointed out that moving government offices out of the former presidential residence demonstrates changes in people's attitude toward protecting cultural relics. ▲ ◄

SHELI PAGODA OF QIXIA MONASTERY
棲霞寺舍利塔

Located behind the Qixia Monastery northeast of Nanjing, this pagoda is said to be where Emperor Wen of the Sui dynasty, founded in AD 581, kept the Sheli (Sarira) cremation remains of the Buddha. He is said to have built it in 601, and it was renovated three centuries later by two chief ministers of the Tang court. The pagoda features eight carved panels depicting the life of Sakyamuni from his descent from heaven: entering the womb, development in the womb, birth, earthly travels, enlightenment, preaching, defeating demons and final transition to Nirvana. ◀

NARROW WEST LAKE (SHOUXIHU)
瘦西湖

Five beautiful yellow-glazed tiled pavilions stand on a 15-arched bridge in Narrow West Lake in Yangzhou, Jiangsu Province, built by a salt merchant in 1757 to commemorate a visit by the Qing emperor Qianlong. It is also called Lotus Blossom Bridge because it was built on a bed of lotus plants, and for many years it has been a popular spot for one of the favorite traditional pastimes of the Chinese, viewing the moon and its reflection on still waters. The White Pagoda stands within the nearby Lianxing Monastery and is a copy of the White Pagoda in Beijing's Beihai Park. It is said that the salt merchant had it built in one single night to impress the visiting emperor—a story that is taken with a grain of salt. ▶

WANGSHIYUAN
網師園

Suzhou (Soochow) has for centuries been known as one of central China's most beautiful cities and the place where wealthy mandarins, merchants and landowners built fine retirement residences, many of them connected to the network of lakes and canals that have given the city the reputation of being the Venice of the East. Wangshiyuan, a particularly well-designed and opulent garden home, was built by Shi Zhengzhi of the Song dynasty and was named Ten Thousand Volumes Hall at first. In 1736 it was bought by Song Zongyuan, who changed its name to Fisherman's Recluse and chose Wangshi (Master of the Net) as the name of its garden. With its cottages, pavilions, studios and ponds, it embodies all that the wealthy retired required of life—visual pleasure and harmony. ▲

West Garden (Xiyuan)
西園

his palatial residential complex and garden in Liuyuan Street, Suzhou, has a colorful and complicated history. First built between 1522 and 1566 by a retired Ming dynasty mandarin, it was then converted to a monastery by his son; then, in the 19th century, it was demolished and rebuilt in its present form. It still includes the monastery, and a main hall that houses the images of 500 arhats and a statue of the monk Ji Gong, whose face, viewed from the right, has an amused, happy expression, but from the left is sad. Viewed from the front, it appears to be happy and sad all at once. The pond that links the various buildings is well stocked with colorful carp and is home to a tortoise said to be over 300 years old. ◀

Zhuozheng Garden
拙政園

Another famous Suzhou residence, the Zhuozheng (Simple Life) Garden, was built in 1513 by a retired civil servant, Wang Xianchen, on the site of the former Dahong Monastery. He took its name from a poem on leisurely living by Pan Yue of the Jin dynasty, a line from which goes: "To water the garden and grow vegetables is a form of government by the simple soul." Renovated in the Qing reign, this is now the largest and most splendid residential garden in Suzhou. Since its first occupant, it has had some illustrious owner-residents, including the grandfather of the novelist Cao Xueqin (author of *Dream of the Red Mansion*) and Li Xiucheng, a leader of the Taiping Rebellion against Manchu rule. ▲

JINSHAN (GOLD HILL) MONASTERY
金山寺

This elegant monastery in Zhenjiang City in Jiangsu was first built in the Eastern Jin dynasty (AD 317–420). During the later Tang rule, gold was discovered there and the monastery's name was changed to Gold Hill. Its dominant pagoda was first erected as one of the twin structures in the Song dynasty. One was later destroyed, and the present pagoda is the result of reconstruction in 1900. Among the monastery's valued relics are the Four Treasures of Jinshan, a bronze tripod of the Zhou dynasty (770–221 BC), a battle drum said to have been used by the Shu Han tactician Zhuge Liang in the Three Kingdoms conflict, a Song dynasty jade belt belonging to the famous bard Su Dongpo and a painting by the Ming dynasty artist Wen Zhengming. ▲

TAI LAKE
太湖

The Tai Lake is the third biggest freshwater lake in China and is famous for its rocks—strange and somewhat bizarre natural formations that have been used all over China to decorate parks and gardens. It is also where Fan Li, the mastermind who helped the Prince of Yue to inflict vengeance on the Prince of Wu in 476 BC, is said to have celebrated his victory by taking the most coveted beauty of that time, Xi Shi, for a boat ride. The lake covers 926 sq. mi. (2400 sq. km) and spreads into the provinces of Jiangsu and Zhejiang. It is fed by two streams, the Tai and Jing, and empties through four others into the Yangtze River. There are 48 small islands in its waters, and the peaks of 72 hills parade around it. ▶

BAODAI BRIDGE
寶帶橋

The Baodai (or Precious Belt) Bridge, 4 mi. (7 km) southeast of Suzhou, is believed to have been given its name when the prefect of Suzhou sold his precious belt to raise funds toward the cost of its construction in AD 806. It is thought to have been built first of wood, then rebuilt with stone in 1232. Just over 600 years later it was rebuilt, taking on the design that it features today. The bridge is 1040 ft. (317 m) long and has 53 arches, three of them large enough to allow junks or river launches and barges through. When the full moon is reflected on the water under each of the arches, it is said to look like a string of 53 moons, or a belt of bright jade. ◀

HANSHAN (COLD MOUNTAIN) MONASTERY
寒山寺

Cold Mountain Monastery in Fengqiao, Suzhou, dates back to AD 502–519 but was destroyed by fire several times over the centuries, and its present structure goes back only to the beginning of this century. Its name is said to have come from the monk Hanshan, who came to the area with a colleague, Shide. Gilded statues of both men are housed in its great hall. The Tang dynasty poet Zhang Ji immortalized the monastery in lines that spoke of "the sound of the midnight bell (coming) to my lonely boat." The monastery bell disappeared a long time ago, and a replacement installed in the Ming dynasty has also gone— it is now in a collection in Japan. A new one hangs in Hanshan monastery, which was made in Japan and donated to the monastery. ▲

THE TIGER HILL (HUQIU) PAGODA
虎丘塔

Built in the middle of the 10th century on Tiger Hill in Suzhou, this eight-sided seven-tiered tapering pagoda is constructed of bricks but in the style of traditional wooden structures. In 700 years, from the 12th to 19th centuries, it suffered seven major fires that badly damaged the top and all the eaves. What remains now is the basic brick structure, which requires constant maintenance. First named the Yunyan Pagoda, it is probably the oldest of its design south of the Yangtze River. The pagoda stands 164 ft. (50 m) high, and every floor is accessible by a wooden staircase.

On every story of the pagoda, there are murals of peonies. Other features, such as the cantilevered brackets and coffered ceilings, are also painted over with rather special designs. ▼

Zhou Zhuang
周莊

The timeless beauty of an arched bridge or a boat gracefully gliding by that brought fame to the city of Venice surprisingly has a number of Chinese counterparts. Created over 700 years ago as a retreat for the wealthy from the cares of government and commerce, Zhou Zhuang is smaller than the nearby more famous water city of Suzhou, but a visit to this charming tiny gem provides the chance to compare the pleasures of a Chinese water town with world famous ones such as Venice and Amsterdam. In Zhou Zhuang, a visitor can tour a number of residences, see performances on a traditional stage and glide through the narrow canals aboard a small boat. The small shops lining the canals that once catered to the needs of the well-to-do now display an impressive variety of China's handcrafts. The gourmet specialty of the town, ham simmered in soy sauce and spices, is found everywhere. Meals can be eaten in large second-story restaurants with views of the waterways or in private homes with the attraction of home-cooked food. Villagers dressed in local peasant style are a living part of the Zhou Zhuang setting as they make some of the most charming craft items in open workshops. Other villagers happily sing the old folksongs to visitors for a small fee. A visit to Zhou Zhuang fuels the imagination and provides a living model for one of the favorite subjects of Chinese artists. ▼

Wuzhen

烏鎮

Little Wuzhen in Jiangsu Province is a small, picturesque town near Hangzhou. It was built along a river. The old two-story houses, some from the Ming and Qing dynasties, look out on the river and are built with a timber framework well preserved with many coats of tung oil, black tile roofs and whitewashed walls. The ground floor of the houses are covered in square brick, an unusual feature in southern China in that era. There are also a number of larger villas, with gardens and family halls, that once belonged to local families of long ago. One of these houses, the Wuzhen Folklore Museum, features displays of local customs for celebrating weddings, birthdays and festivals. The town center has the traditional high stage where many local talents perform Shaoxing, Peking and flower-drum operas. The scene is as it has always been, relaxed and chatty, with townsfolk coming and going during the lengthy performances. The town also has one of the most famous Taoist temples in southern China. Visitors can wander the town enjoying the workshop area, where local specialties such as Sanbai wine, cloth shoes, cakes and bamboo items are made and sold. Famous local teas are served in teahouses, and visitors can sample the typical Wuzhen-style braised chicken seasoned with soy sauce in the restaurants. ▼

WEST LAKE OF HANGZHOU
杭州西湖

The West Lake was called Golden Cow Lake before the Song dynasty because a golden cow was said to materialize on its waters whenever a sage or holy man passed by. Later, the poet Su Shi (Dongpo) compared the lake with the famous beauty Xi Shi, writing that like the courtesan, "it is attractive with make-up or without." The lake site used to be a shallow bay connected to the Qiantang River but was gradually sealed off by alluvial deposit, and dredging and landscaping did the rest.

This oval-shaped lake has an area of about 2.3 sq. mi. (6 sq. km) and a circumference of 9.3 mi. (15 km). The average depth of the lake is about 5 ft. (1.5 m), with the deepest part being only 9 ft. (2.8 m) and the shallowest spot less than 3.3 ft. (1 m).

The city of Hangzhou stands on its eastern shore. On the gentle slopes of the hills surrounding the three sides of the lake are large gardens displaying a variety of flora: peach blossom in spring, lily in summer, osmanthus in autumn and plum blossom in winter. The hills are dotted with pavilions, pagodas, grottoes, mansions and streams.

The lake also adds its beauty and mystique to the Ten Beautiful Sights of Hangzhou—Autumn Moon over the Smooth Lake, Spring Dawn over the Su Bridge, Snow over the Broken Bridge, Dusk at the Thunder Peak Pagoda, Evening Bell from Nanping, Waving Lotuses on a Garden Pond, Golden Carp in Huagang, Listening to the Nightingales under Willows on Lakeside, Moon Reflected on the Three Ponds and Double Peaks Piercing the Clouds.

Apart from being a scenic spot, the lake supplies water for irrigation and is rich in aquatic products. ▲

LIUHE PAGODA
六和塔

The Liuhe Pagoda, also known as Six Harmonies Pagoda, stands on the Qiantang River in Hangzhou and was first erected in AD 970 in the belief that it would help placate mischievous spirits and control local flooding. The present brick pagoda was built in 1153, and its wooden eaves were renovated in 1899. The octagonal pagoda is nearly 200 ft. (60 m) high, with 104 iron windbells playing from the corners of its eaves. ▲

GRAVE OF YUE FEI
岳墳

General Yue Fei, the Song dynasty military chief who was wrongly accused and put to death by his political rival, Qin Hui, was originally buried on Hangzhou's North Hill, but his tomb was moved to Qixia Hill beside the West Lake in 1163. Near the entrance to the tomb, there stands a pavilion called Zhongbai (Loyal Cedar), housing a petrified cedar tree. It is said to have suddenly died when the general was executed. Nearby is the Temple of General Yue, which was once known as Zhonglie (Loyal Martyr) Temple. The present building is the result of renovation in the Qing dynasty. ▶

TEMPLE OF GENERAL YUE

岳王廟

Two rows of red-lacquered pillars lead to the main hall of the Temple of General Yue, each engraved with scenes of his most famous Song dynasty battles against Jin invaders. Another engraving displays the characters Xin Zhao Tian Ri (Heart as Clear as Sun in Sky), based on the general's last words before execution. The seated statue of the great warrior was only recently cast and installed. Over it hangs a plaque inscribed with four Chinese characters Huan Wo He Shan (Restore to Us Our Land and Rivers), and the ceiling is painted with more than 370 white cranes, symbolizing loftiness and staunch loyalty.

▲

Lingyin Monastery
靈隱寺

This famous monastery stands to the northwest of the West Lake in Hangzhou. Its site was selected in AD 326 (Eastern Jin dynasty) by the Indian abbot Huili, who decided it was a fitting "hermitage for the Immortals." During the Five Dynasties following the collapse of Han rule, the devoutly Buddhist Zian Liu, the prince of Yue, greatly expanded the monastery to include nine mansions, 18 pavilions and 3000 monks and novices. When the Qing emperor Kangxi visited the huge complex on his trip to southern China, he gave it the name Cloud Forest Zen Monastery (Yunlin Chansi). The monastery still features its ornate Great Hall, a 110-ft. (33.6-m) high structure that houses a 30-ft. (9.1-m) tall gilded statue of Sakyamuni Buddha sitting on a lotus pedestal, based on a well-known sculpture of the Tang dynasty. A lengthy couplet describing famous scenic spots in Hangzhou is inscribed on two tall pillars in front of the statue. The hall is also decked with other images and paintings representing Buddhist mythology, and two ancient stone plaques with inscriptions from the scriptures. ◄

Feilai Peak Stone Carvings
飛來峰石刻

There are as many as 300 stone carvings that adorn the walls and caves of Feilai (Flown Here) Peak near the Lingyin Monastery. The most well-known sculpture is that of Maitreya in the form of the Laughing Buddha. Its name comes from the monastery's founder, the Indian monk Huili, who is said to have commented on a visit there: "This looks like a hill of the Immortal Vulture Mountain of Tianzhu. I wonder when it flew and settled here." The sculptures shown here were begun in the Five Dynasties period (AD 907–960) and added to in the reigns of the Song and Mongol Yuan. ►

YANDANG MOUNTAIN

雁蕩山

Yandang Mountain is situated in Leqing County, Zhejiang. The leading peak, Yanhugang (Wild Goose Lake Peak), lies 3432 ft. (1046 m) above sea level. It was so named because wild geese reside in the lake on the peak, where reeds and rushes flourish. The igneous rocks give the mountain its rugged appearance and a tint of red. The mountain has been a favorite of poets and painters, providing them with inspiration for poems, paintings and travels. Some of the artists who visited the mountain include Xie Lingyun the poet, Shen Kuo the Song dynasty scholar, Tang Yin the painter and Xu Xiake the veteran traveler of the Ming dynasty. Its popularity is not surprising, since the towering fortress-like peaks and cliffs embrace more than 360 scenic spots. The sheer faces have provided sanctuary and safety for Buddhism as well, and there are many ruins of old monasteries among its peaks. ▲

EAST LAKE OF SHAOXING
紹興東湖

This lake, along with the West Lake of Hangzhou and the South Lake of Jiaxing, are together known as the three great lakes of eastern Zhejiang. Its long dyke was built during the final Qing dynastic reign to separate its waters from those of the Grand Canal. Bridges and pavilions were also erected and the lakeside beautified with peach and willow trees. Nine stone bridges span the lake, dividing it into three sections. On its shores there are two caves that have for many years been popular tourist spots—Xiantao (Immortal Peach) and Taogong caves, both of which can be reached by boat. A stone column at Immortal Peach Cave is inscribed with a couplet that says the "cave is deeper than five hundred feet / The peach trees blossom every three thousand years"—a gross exaggeration, but a nice one. ▶

PUTUO MOUNTAIN

普陀山

Taking its name from a Sanskrit term meaning "beautiful white flower," Putuo Mountain lies on an island-county of the same name to the east of Zhoushan archipelago. Legend has it that the goddess Guanyin appeared here once, and since then it has been one of the four great Buddhist mountain retreats of China. A group of precariously balanced boulders proclaim the mountain's importance in big red characters that read Sea-Sky-Buddha Kingdom.

It is said that in AD 916 a Japanese monk set off from Wutai Mountain to carry an image of Guanyin back to his country. When he reached Putuo Mountain, he was caught in the winds of a typhoon, so he built a monastery there dedicated to "Guanyin who will not leave." This was probably the first of the many monasteries built on Putuo Mountain. In 1214 an edict was issued ordering that Guanyin should be the principal object of worship there. In its heyday, Putuo Mountain had more than 300 monasteries, temples and shrines. Pu Ji, Fa Yu and Hui Ji Monasteries are the three most renowned monastic buildings. Pu Ji Monastery is the principal monastery devoted to the worship of Guanyin. Hui Ji Monastery was greatly expanded in 1907 upon the acquisition of a set of the

Tripitaka sutra. The monastic architecture set against the ever-changing seascape is best described by Wang Anshi of the Song dynasty: "Lightly the clouds saunter over the hills on the sea. Here is a world away from the mundane world." ◄ ▼

THE YANGTZE RIVER

長江

Also known as Changjiang, or Long River, the Yangtze River begins its 3915-mi. (6300-km) surge to the distant East China Sea as the trickling runoff of melting snows in the Tanggula Mountains in western Qinghai (below). As it gathers its immense volume, it traverses Tibet, Yunnan, Sichuan, Hubei, Hunan, Jiangxi, Anhui and Jiangsu, carving itself deeply into the terrain, collecting over 700 tributaries, and draining a basin of nearly 772,000 sq. mi. (2,000,000 sq. km)—almost 20 percent of China's total land space.

The river can be divided into three main sections. The upper section, called Jinshajiang, ends at Yibin in Sichuan. This stretch measures about 2175 mi. (3500 km). At Yibin, it joins Minjiang to become Changjiang.

The middle section takes a zigzag course and runs for about 621 mi. (1000 km), cutting through the Sichuan Basin and the gorges of the hilly terrain of Hubei. The Three Gorges of the Yangtze are found in this section where the water reaches savage speed.

The lower section is much wider and more slow moving. However, there are a series of sharp turns and twists in the gorges between Hubei and Hunan called the Nine Curved Intestine. Many lakes are also located in this section, the largest being Dongting, a natural reservoir of the Yangtze River.

The river is probably the most important communication link in China, joining east and west and the northern provinces with those of the south. Its fertile basin supports about 400 million people, just under a third of China's total population. Over 49,710 mi. (80,000 km) of its main waterways and tributaries are navigable. Ships of more than 10,000 tons can go up the river as far as Nanjing and smaller vessels to Hankou, Chongqing and Yibin. If the Yellow River to the north is associated with the birth and early settlement of China, the Yangtze and its vast basin became the vital strategic prize, without which no conqueror or ruler could ever hold sway over China for long. The Yangtze is not only a huge river, third largest in the world after the Amazon and Nile, it is also one of the fiercest and most powerful rivers.

Tuotuo River

If one adopts the principle that the source of a river should be traced to its most remote spot, then the source of the Yangtze is the snow-fed Tuotuo River, 16,405–19,686 ft. (5000–6000 m) up in the Tanggula Mountain Range of Qinghai. The Tuotuo flows northward initially, and after passing through a valley, it crashes through the Heman Rapids, then broadens out over wide pebbled beds before reaching Hulu Lake and deflecting eastwards and widening again. The mighty Yangtze has begun. Before the Ming dynasty, it was thought that Minjiang or the Min River fed the Yangtze, but it is now commonly recognized that this high-mountain runoff is in fact the source. ▲

First Bend of the Yangtze River

About 43 mi. (70 km) west of Lijiang, the ancient Naxis town famed for its sturdy wooden houses, the Yangtze River dramatically changes course to the north and begins its long journey through China as one of the country's great rivers. The origins of the Yangtze River are in the Tangula Mountains of northern Tibet. From there its course follows the Henghuan range before entering the area where it is called the Jinshajiang, which means Golden Sand River. The Yangtze's sudden northward change in direction is called the First Bend and is a location of great importance in Chinese history.

The small town called Stone Drum is cradled in that bend that sends the river north, and it has existed at least since the Ming dynasty. Crossing the Yangtze at the First Bend has long been a strategic military maneuver requiring great skill. Over 1500 years ago, the famous military strategist Zhuge Liang crossed the Yangtze River, as did Kublai Khan a thousand years later, using inflated sheepskin bags. More recently, in 1936, as part of the celebrated Long March, the retreating Red Army of 18,000 soldiers crossed at the First Bend on their way to safety in the north.

After the turn north, the Yangtze rushes through a narrow 9-mi. (15-km) gorge that is nearly 10,000 ft. (3000 m) deep. Called Hutiao Gorge, which means Jumping Tiger, the gorge's name comes from the ancient legend of a hunted tiger that, with the aid of a giant boulder in the middle of the river, jumped the narrowest 98 ft. (30 m) of the gorge to escape his pursuers. ▼

Shibaozhai

Shaped like a Chinese jade seal, with hanging cliffs on all four sides, the hill on which Shibaozhai stands is called Jade Seal Hill. Rising abruptly from the bank of the Yangtze, this hill affords yet another scenic spot on the river's middle course. Shibaozhai is the name of the remarkable structure that crowns this hill. Essentially a fort, it consists of a gate located on the bank of the river, a 12-story tower leading from the gate to the hilltop, and a monastery that stands at the top. The entire structure measures 197 ft. (60 m) in height and is built into the contours of the hill in wood and stone. Constructed during the reign of the Qing emperor Kangxi (1662–1723), it boasts many stone plaques with famous inscriptions. The bottom of the tower is immerged in the water after the damming of the river. ▶

Baidi Hill

This broad terraced hill, lying in the eastern part of Sichuan's Fengjie County, is where the Yangtze flows into 120 mi. (193 km) of deep gorges and jagged rapids. Because of its position, it has always been of great strategic value, and many battles have been fought for control of it over the centuries. Beyond Baidi Hill, the Yangtze hits the Jutang Gorges, down which the Tang dynasty poet Li Bai took a hair-raising ride, describing how "On both sides of the river the gibbons cry incessantly / As the light skiff speeds past hills on hills." ▶

Shennufeng

This former glacier, one of the 12 peaks of the Wu Mountains, stands on the north bank of the Wu Gorge overlooking the Yangtze in Sichuan's Wushan County. Its name means "goddess," and it is said that from a distance it looks like a girl standing in a graceful pose. It is also called Wangxia Peak, or Looking at Colored Clouds Peak, because it is the tallest in the area and therefore is the first to catch the sunrise and the last to reflect the setting sun.

In ancient Chinese mythology, the daughter of Xiwangmu, the Heavenly Mother, is said to have descended from heaven to help the ancient ruler Yu, who was charged with the mission of controlling the great deluge that was sweeping over all of China. After giving him written instructions on the methods he should employ, she decided to remain on earth and dwell on this peak, and was later buried on the southern slope of Wu Mountain. Many poetic works depicted her as a fairy beauty involved in romance with mortal beings, and a temple is devoted to her worship in the county town nearby. ◀

Jutang Gorge

This, the shortest of the so-called Three Gorges of the Yangtze, is also the most dramatic. Its mouth is very narrow, less than 328 ft. (100 m) across, with steep walls on both sides, and the Tang dynasty poet Du Fu described it aptly when he wrote of it as the gate through which all the waters of Sichuan battle to gain access. Another poet, Bai Juyi, came up with this description: "The banks are like two screens kept ajar, through which the sky peeks." Yet another bard, unnamed, created an even more rhapsodic vision: "The tops of the cliffs touch the sky; the boat seems to navigate underground." Guarding the mouth of the gorge are two mountains—Tuzi Mountain (Pear Mountain) on the left and Bai Yan Mountain (White Salt Mountain) on the right.

Two iron poles are embedded in the rock on both sides of the gorge and are said to have been put there by Zhang Wu in the year AD 904. According to records of the Five Dynasties era, Zhang installed iron chains between the poles to regulate traffic on the river. The idea behind this was defense, but in later periods the barrier was used to extract tolls from passing river tradesmen.

On the cliff of Bai Yan Mountain, a series of holes drilled through the rock runs in a zigzag line down from the peak until it reaches the foot of the mountain. These are the remains of the wooden footpath used by the ancient herb collectors.

In a steep wall on the north bank, there are a number of neatly carved rectangular caves, which are believed to have contained the remains of nobles of the Warring States period. Nine "hanging coffins" have been found, containing human bones and bronze swords. The tiny tombs are similar to those of the Toraja mountain tribe in South Sulawesi, Indonesia, who not only buried their nobles in specially cut niches in cliffs but also installed lifelike, fully clothed wooden effigies of them. ▼

Wu Gorge

Wu Gorge is the most picturesque of the Three Gorges of the Yangtze, a scenic picture gallery cutting more than 25 mi. (40 km) through the main ridge of Wu Mountain. Xu Rulong of the Qin dynasty became enthusiastic about the scene, writing, "As I put out my boat in the Wu Gorge my heart is with the twelve peaks"—referring to the 12 mountain summits that range around the narrow waterway. In the *Song of the Three Gorges*, the Song dynasty poet Lu You spoke of how "over the bow of my boat a green splendor fills the autumn air." Other literary tributes ranged from the peaks "floating in the purple void" to "precariously hanging in the blue vault." Beneath one particular peak, Jixian (Gathering Immortals), the scene is described with crushing simplicity in an inscription that reads, "Multiple-Cliffs-and-Piled-Up-Hills Wu Gorge." ◀

Xiling Gorge

Spanning a distance of 44 mi. (70 km) between Sichuan and Hubei Provinces, the Xiling Gorge is the longest of the three, and it was once the most dangerous before Gezhouba Dam was built. There used to be not only narrow passages bristling with half-submerged rocks but a series of severe rapids too, including the perilous Kongling Rapids, which a local folk song had described as the "demon's gate." In the past, the stretch of white water was risky enough when the level of the river was low and its rocks were exposed like jagged teeth, but when the Yangtze was swollen and they were submerged, they were an even greater danger to the hulls of river craft. All this thrill is gone after the damming of the river in Yichang, Hubei Province. ▼

Shanghai

Shanghai, the largest city in China, is located at the mouth of the Yangtze River. Its phenomenal growth in the last 15 years is the talk of Asia and the entire world. The start of the boom began in 1990, and now it seems the skyline of the city changes every month. In the '20s and '30s of the last century, Shanghai was known as the Paris of the East, but upheaval and war intervened. Now Shanghai has regained its luster, luring people from all over the world to visit and invest. Shanghai today is a place "where yesterday meets tomorrow."

Pudong, literally east of the (Huang Pu) river across from the Bund (opposite, bottom), most exemplifies the dramatic changes in Shanghai. Ten years ago Pudong was mostly rice and vegetable fields, but today it is Shanghai's newest industrial and residential area, fanning out from Lujiazui (above), the finance and trade center of the metropolis, all the way to the East China Sea.

In the old city area, large public parks have been created, and colonial-period neighborhoods, known as Shikumen, with '30s' row houses, have been refurbished to help preserve the flavor of an earlier era. Shanghai's downtown showpiece, Xintiandi (New Heaven and Earth, below), is the chic area in the city center, with trendy shops, restaurants and cafés for locals and visitors alike. ▲ ▼

DETIAN WATERFALL OF GUANGXI

The Southern Region

The southern region of China, which covers the provinces of Yunnan, Guizhou, Guangdong, Guangxi, Fujian and Taiwan, is not noted for its role in the vanguard of Chinese history. Yet it was one of the first areas of China to trade with the outside world and was the scene of a bitter 19th-century struggle with the "foreign devil" that ultimately brought the age-old dynastic tradition to an end. It was the power struggle in the so-called Opium War of 1839–42, centered on the thriving trading concession at Guangzhou (Canton), that saw the British Navy defeat China's imperial war junks, grab the island of Hong Kong and a slice of mainland territory as a colony and open the way for an international "carveup" of Chinese sovereignty that the weakened, antiquated Manchu Qing dynasty could not effectively resist.

Physically the region is divided into the highlands of Yunnan and Guizhou and the lowland areas of the other provinces. These in turn are dotted with abrupt, weirdly shaped towers and cones of limestone, giving Guilin in particular its unique and long-renowned beauty, and poets and painters a fountainhead of inspiration. Fast-flowing rivers crisscross the region, gouging deep gorges in the karst terrain—as deep as 10,000 ft. (3000 m) in the highland areas—and the landscape also features huge caves, underground rivers, "stone forests" and red sandstone terraces. The climate ranges from subtropical to tropical and is influenced along the coastal areas by both the monsoon and the dreaded typhoon—powerful hurricane-force anticyclones that boil up out of the Pacific south of the Philippines and surge north to dash themselves, one after the other, on the south China coast.

Though not very outstanding historically, the region is noted for the discovery in Yunnan of the oldest-known bronze drum, dating from the 5th century BC. One of China's great irrigation systems was built in Guangxi during the short but crucial Qin reign (221–207 BC). There are monuments in Yunnan—the Three Pagodas of Dali City, Stone Bell Hill and the monasteries of Chicken Feet Mountain—that are a legacy of the province's political importance between the 8th and 13th centuries. The Guangxiao Monastery in Guangdong Province dates back to the 3rd century BC. Perhaps the greatest of the region's legacies, however, is the role it played for centuries as a refuge for scholar mandarins who had lost favor in the imperial courts.

The region is also famous for being the flashpoint of rebellion, the last and greatest of these being the republican campaign against the Manchus led by the sons and daughters of southern merchants and officials who, like the region itself, had become more modernized and therefore more progressive in thought than China's northern areas through contact with foreign traders, teachers and missionaries.

DIQING WHITE RESERVOIR
迪慶白水塘

This long, narrow terraced valley floor lies between snowcapped mountain peaks in the Yunnan highlands and is typical of the "wild beauty" of much of the southern region—largely the result of water erosion on the karst or limestone terrain. Clear streams cascade down the white and pinkish steps that the waters have carved and sculpted over millions of years. Geologists believe that most of the southern region was once under water, and a tumultuous rise in the earth's crust threw up the limestone plate that covers most of the area. ▼

LIJIANG
麗江

The old town area in Lijiang probably has the greatest number of timber houses still in their original Naxi village setting in China. Visitors can wander the narrow cobblestone streets while admiring the Naxi-style timber houses. The cleverly engineered water system taps a clean water source high in the mountains above Lijiang, channeling streams to the town to bring water to the residents along each street and to the neighborhood pit wells designated for drinking water, vegetable washing and clothes washing. Each timber house is beautifully decorated with carvings. They are not built to delight the eye only. When a strong earthquake destroyed most masonry buildings of recent construction in Lijiang and killed 300 people in 1996, most of the timber houses of the Naxi withstood the quake with little damage. In tribute to the ingenious local Naxi architecture, the government decided to rebuild with timber structures. An evening stroll might allow the lucky visitor to watch a Naxi folk dance. There are opportunities to learn about the religious beliefs of the Naxi and to visit one of the tallest wooden pagodas in China, carved with Dongba scripture. Only the shamans of the Naxi are

taught to read and write the more than 1000 Dongba pictographs.

High above Lijiang towers the Jade Dragon Snow Mountain, which is really a mountain range 22 mi. (35 km) long. The tallest of these breathtaking peaks is Shanzidou or Fan Peak at over 18,360 ft. (5596 m). Although difficult to climb, Fan Peak was finally scaled in 1963. ▲ ▲

Tiger Jump Gorge

Another typical feature of the landscape in the western mountain areas of the south, this gorge cuts through hills 10,000 ft. (3000 m) or higher northeast of Lijiang County in the southern province of Yunnan. Its waters are part of the Jinsha River. They rush, twisting and turning, for 9 mi. (15 km) through the deep valley. A large boulder stands at the narrowest point of the gorge, and it is here that the area was given its name. It is said that a tiger, pursued by hunters, saved itself in the nick of time by jumping from the boulder to the opposite bank. ▶

Black Dragon Pond

Black Dragon Pond (Heilongtan), with its beautiful triple-eaved Fayun Pavilion and the elegant carved stone balustrade of its bridge, is thought to have existed as early as the Han dynasty. It lies at the foot of Elephant Hill in Lijiang County. The pond is also called Jade Fountain because of a temple nearby, built in the time of the Ming, that goes by the name of Jade Fountain Dragon King. ▼

LAKE DIAN
滇池

Otherwise known as Kunming Lake, this narrow stretch of water, 25 mi. (40 km) long and 5 mi. (8 km) wide, lies southwest of the city. Its upper reaches form an area of dense reeds and rushes called West Lake, or Little Sea of Grass. The lake lies close to Kunming's West Mountains, a chain of hills in the shape of a girl reclining on her side—named, not surprisingly, Sleeping Beauty Mountain. There is a legend that tells of the birth of both the lake and the mountains. A fisherman's daughter was in love with a young man who, one day, disappeared in a violent storm. She wept so much that her tears formed the lake and she herself became Sleeping Beauty Mountain.

This area was apparently populated as long ago as the 3rd century BC, the time of the Warring States, and ancient tombs have been excavated in the vicinity. Famous scenic spots, such as the Grand Mansion and Zhenghe Park, line the shores of the lake. ▶

Dragon Gate (Longmen)

This remarkable complex of paths and caves, cut high in the side of a sheer cliff, derived its name from the mythological tale of the ancient hero Yu who opened up Dragon Gate to curb the deluge.

In actual history, the creation of this scenic spot is no less legendary. The path and grottoes took 72 years to carve out of the rock, beginning in 1781 in the reign of the Qing emperor Qianlong. Then a sculptor named Zhu Jiage spent eight years carving various images to decorate the main cave hall, including a statue of the god of literature. One day a pen brush he was shaping in the figure's hand broke off. Zhu was so mortified that he leaped from the precipice to his death. Today a tourist can thread his way up through the pavilions, caves and gates until he reaches the top, an act that in the past symbolized scholarly achievement in the imperial examinations. ◀

GRAND MANSION (DAGUANLOU)
大觀樓

This airy, palatial, square pavilion–shaped mansion stands on an island outside Kunming city on the northern tip of Lake Dian. Aside from its splendid architecture and setting, its main feature is a famous couplet that decorates its main doors—it consists of 180 Chinese characters, 90 on each door, and is reputed to be the longest couplet ever written. The mansion was built in 1682 and was first called Buddha Temple. Two centuries later it was renovated and beautified with bridges, willows, dikes and galleries. Lake Dian, covering an area of 131 sq. mi. (340 sq. km), is the sixth largest freshwater lake in China. ▼

THE STONE FOREST (SHILIN)
雲南石林

One of the natural marvels of China, the Stone Forest in Yunnan is believed to have been formed in two stages—by the earth's crust pushing up above waters that are believed to have covered the southern region in pre-history, and then by the erosive action of wind and rain on the limestone outcrops. Under the ground, erosion by sub-terranean water has also created huge caves. Some of the columns rise as high as 131 ft. (40 m) and are linked by natural stone corridors and hanging bridges. Various spots have been given descriptive names, such as Big Stone Forest, Small Stone Forest, Long Lake, Moon Lake, Lion Hill, Layered Waterfall and Sword Blade Pool (left), where a swordlike stone peak rises dramatically out of the water. Footpaths and pavilions have been added to guide visitors through this bizarre maze, which has been the source of many fairy legends. ◀ ▼

YUANTONG MONASTERY

圓通寺

Yuantong (Enlightenment) Monastery was constructed between 1301 and 1320 in the northeast district of Kunming. It is an ornate complex, standing on the side of a small lake and featuring an elegant triple-arched stone bridge. Pictured right is the pailou, or main arch, of the monastery. One of the monastery's main buildings is an eight-cornered pavilion, featuring a touch of the 20ᵗʰ-century decorative lights on its roof. The monastery lies at the foot of Yuantong Hill, the highest viewpoint in Kunming. ▶

THE YUANMOU EARTH FOREST

土林

The Yuanmou Earth Forest lies about 124 mi. (200 km) from the provincial capital Kunmin, yet its spectacular karst rocks weren't known to the public until mid-1980s. For years that area has been known as the treasure house for fossilized ancient living things, such as the fossilized Lufeng ramapithecus about 8 million years ago, Yuanmou Man (Homo Erectus Yuanmouensis) about 1.7 million years ago and Lufeng dinosaurs of 1.8 billion years ago. Now the 13 earth forests are one of the main attractions of this 17-sq.-mi. (42-sq.-km) Yuanmou Basin, which consists of three scenic spots: Xinghua, Bangguo and Tiger Jumping Beach. Its landscape was formed by geological movement and soil erosion 1 or 2 million years

ago. The karst rocks look like castles, screens and fossilized trees, some as high as 131 ft. (40 m), hence the name of the area. ▲

TERRACED FIELDS
哀牢山梯田

So much of China is hills and mountains and so huge is its population—around 1.3 billion people, a quarter of the world's total population, and about 64 percent of them working on the land—that the demand for agricultural land is enormous. For centuries, hillsides have been terraced and cultivated for the farming of rice, tea, cotton and a variety of other agricultural produce. Yunnan Province is so short of lowland area that terraces are widely distributed in the highlands east of Ailao Mountain.

Some of these terraces are cut into slopes that rise as high as 2000 m. The slopes are leveled into horizontal strips, with low earthen walls lining the outer edges, thus facilitating irrigation and preventing soil erosion. Spreading out from the areas of denser population—town settlements locally known as bazi—these terraced fields form picturesque asymmetrical patterns in different shades of green, yellow and brown, lending color to the landscape. ▼

DALI CITY
大理

Nestled at the foot of Cang Mountain, Dali City was once an important political, economic and cultural center in west Yunnan. It served as the capital for the Nanzhao regime in the Tang dynasty and the Dali regime in the Song dynasty, respectively. The existing layout is of the Ming dynasty, when Dali was rebuilt into a square-shaped city in 1382. Parts of the original walls still remain.

The landmark for Dali is the Three Pagodas of Chongsheng Temple outside the city. Built over a thousand years ago, these elegant and stately brick pagodas are representative of the Bai ethnic style. But most spectacular of all are the 18 creeks that run between the 19 peaks outside Dali and the Jade Belt Clouds that hang on the slopes of Cang Mountain in late summer or early fall, especially after a rainfall.

A mile to the north of the city is the Erhai Lake, meaning "sea shaped like an ear" in Chinese. This crescent-shaped lake is one of the seven largest freshwater lakes in China, covering an area of 97 sq. mi. (250 sq. km). The crystal-clear water of the Erhai Lake and the snow-covered Cang Mountain are commonly described as Silver Cangshan and Jade Erhai. ▲

SHANGRI-LA (ZHONGDIAN)
香格里拉（中甸）

Long known as Zhongdian, this mountainous region in northwestern Yunnan Province was renamed Shangri-La in 2001, after the paradise of peaceful tranquility of snowy mountains, grasslands, Tibetan people and red soil plateaus, vividly described by the British writer James Hilton in his novel *Lost Horizon*. Shangri-La is actually a Tibetan word, which means "land of sacredness and peace." Once this area served as a major caravan stop on the ancient tea trade routes between India, South China and Burma. Shangri-La is located in the heart of the Hengduan Mountain Range, which is rich with many natural attractions, such as Bita Lake Nature Preserve, Napa Lake White Water Terrace, Haba Snow Mountain and Meli Snow Mountain. Shangri-La has a number of ethnic groups besides the Tibetan people. The smaller groups include Naxis, the Lisus and the Yis. Their exotic customs and ancient way of life adds much charm to the area's natural beauty. A vast system of rivers traverses the snow-covered mountains and deep valleys. Typical of the area is the Birang Valley, tucked deep in the mountains. The six-mi.

(10-km) long valley is surrounded by sheer cliffs and at places is over 6000 ft. (2000 m) deep along a narrow valley, very much like the one described in *Lost Horizon*. The deep valleys are flanked by some of the highest mountain peaks in the world. Kagebo Peak, known as the Chief of the Eight Sacred Peaks, soars 22,114 ft. (6740 m), still destined to be conquered by mankind. ▲ ▼

Jiaxiu Mansion

甲秀樓

This three-story wooden mansion with three tiers of green-tiled flying eaves stands in Guiyang City, Guizhou. It was built in 1597 and is noted for its many plaques engraved with literary couplets. ▲

Flower Stream (Huaxi)

花溪

Part of the Nanming River, the Flower Stream is the centerpiece of a public park situated 11 mi. (17 km) south of the town of Guiyang. The banks of this shallow stream are renowned for their lovely scenery of plowed fields and village settlements. In the park, four hills are identified—the Unicorn, the Phoenix, the Tortoise and the Snake, each with outstanding picturesque features such as caves, cliffs, waterfalls, pavilions, bamboo groves, flower beds, bridges on streamlets and boating resorts.

The upper reaches of Flower Stream pass under a stone

bridge that zigzags between the banks, following the path of a weir. Nearby, a string of 100 large stepping stones runs from one bank to the other. In the summer this is a favorite haunt for swimmers, while tourists like to climb the many towers and terraces erected along the shores.

▲

YELLOW FRUIT TREE WATERFALLS
黃果樹瀑布

Close to Rhinoceros Cave, this waterfall, the largest in China, spans a width of 98–131 ft. (30–40 m) and thunders 197 ft. (60 m) down into Rhinoceros Pool, a cascade almost equaling the size and power of Niagara Falls on the United States–Canadian border. The waterfall derived its name from the "yellow fruit tree" (tangerine) plantations found upstream of the River Baishui, which at this point in Guizhou's Zhenning County descends the hill-slopes in nine steps, this waterfall being the highest and most dramatic.

A pavilion on the opposite cliff commands a full view of the cascade, and in a stalactite cave below, spectators can watch the magnificent downpour through three openings. It is claimed that the roar of the falling water can be heard some 3 mi. (5 km) away. ▲

283

QIANLING MOUNTAIN
黔靈山

Heavily wooded and rising over a large lake, this gentle mountain range sprawls through the northwestern area of Guizhou Province. It has many hills, the most noted of them being Elephant Hill, White Elephant Hill and Sandalwood Hill. Near the lake, the karst rock has been eroded by an underground stream to form a big cavern called Unicorn Cave. ▼

Hongfu Monastery

This pretty but relatively modest monastery stands at the summit of Qianling Mountain in Guizhou and is noted for its statues of the Sakyamuni and Maitreya Buddhas, the goddess Guanyin and Guanyu, the God of War. Emperor Guan, as he is also known, is one of China's most popular gods and is said to be a deified military hero from Shanxi Province, who raised an army and suppressed a rebellion in the late Han dynasty. Later he was taken prisoner and executed by a rival warlord, but his spirit is said to have continued to work for the protection of the nation, and in 1594 he was officially declared a god. ◀

DRUM TOWER OF EAST GUIZHOU
黔東鼓樓

This exquisite wooden building, a drum tower, is characteristic of the traditional architecture of eastern Guizhou Province, which is populated mainly by the Dong clans. The Dong clans group themselves under surnames, and each village has a drum tower that serves as a meeting place, entertainment center and an alarm post. A leather drum is hung from the topmost eave and used to summon village elders for urgent consultation or to raise the entire village in the event of an outside threat. The Dong are also found in Hunan Province and in the Guangxi Zhuang Autonomous Region. ▼

QIFENG TOWN
奇峰鎮

Looking like a scene from a fantasy story, the town of Qifeng (Strange Peaks) lies only 6 mi. (10 km) from the city of Guilin, celebrated throughout China and known throughout most of the rest of the world for the limestone mounds, towers and cones that form its unique natural architecture. The extraordinary blend of placid, flat rice paddies, meandering rivers, lush vegetation and the abrupt tombstone effect of the mounds has challenged poets and painters throughout China's history. One of them, Han Yu, wrote of it: "The river is a turquoise gauze belt, the mountains like a jade clasp." ◄

FUBO HILL
伏波山

Rising up from the bank of the Li River in Guilin, Fubo Hill is one of the most popular hills for tourists and painters alike in the fairyland setting of the karst country. Artists of all persuasions have visited the hill over the centuries, and writers have left their calling cards on it: Among the tributes inscribed on the rock of the hill is a poem by Fan Chengda and a self-portrait by the well-known painter Mi Fu, both from the Song dynasty. ▲

LI RIVER

漓江

Fishermen on bamboo rafts, their lamps lit to attract shoals of fish, add to the fairyland effect of the Li River and its most scenic stretch between Guilin and Yangshuo. The men use tamed cormorants to make their catches. The Li River, a principal tributary of the River Gwei, flows from Xing'an northwest of Guilin through to Yangshuo and then joins the West River after a distance of 272 mi. (437 km).

Its waters are varied. The Guilin-Yangshuo stretch is so placid that one can see the pebbles lying on the riverbed. Elsewhere, the rapids can be difficult to negotiate.

The numerous, rugged peaks on the two sides of the meandering river offer a feast to the river traveler's eye. Yuan Mei, the Qing poet, marveled at the swift-changing scenery and made the following observation of the river tour. "One moment, you see the green peaks floating over your head; the next, they glide under your boat." ◀ ▼

REED PIPE CAVE (LUDIYAN)

蘆笛岩

This magnificent cavern, packed with bizarre rock formations and stalactites and stalagmites, is in the slope of Guangming Mountain, 4 mi. (6 km) north of Guilin City. It was first discovered in antiquity, and inscriptions have been found on its walls dating back at least 1000 years. But somehow, probably because of civil war, it was forgotten for some time and then rediscovered—some say the local people kept it a secret, using it as a convenient hiding place in times of war.

Ludiyan measures 787 ft. (240 m) across and is divided into two sections separated by a pond forming a natural barrier. The cave features a rock called the Old Scholar, named after a sage who is said to have been so enchanted by Guilin's scenery that he began a poem about it—but, unable to conjure up words adequate enough to finish it, he turned to stone.

Other rock formations take the shape of a horse, a lion, a drum or a zither—all uncannily true to life. The cave is illuminated, and visitors are able to take in an enjoyable tour that covers about 1641 ft. (500 m). ▲

FENGYU CAVE
豐魚岩

Located in Shanhe 68 mi. (110 km) southeast of Guilin, Fengyu Cave is a 3.3 mi. (5.3 km) long karst cave with a subterranean river 1.4 mi. (2.3 km) long. It is named after a kind of red fish in the cave river, called Feng Yu. The cave passes 9 karst peaks and has with many large chambers, the biggest of which is more than 274,480 sq. ft. (25,500 sq. m).

First developed in 1994, Fengyu Cave has been a popular and revered showpiece of the Guilin area. The stalagmites in Fengyu Cave are fairly young and are growing quickly. Most of them are slender and some paper thin. One typical stalagmite, named Ding Hai Shen Zhen (Marvelous Needle) is 32 ft. (9.8 m) high but only about 5.9 in. (15 cm) in diameter. The cave can be visited by a 30-minute walk through different rock formations, followed by a boat tour on the underground river. ▼

Yangshuo
陽朔

There is a well-known saying that goes, "The rivers and hills of Guilin are the most beautiful in China, and those of Yangshuo surpass Guilin's."

Certainly, the contrast of limestone and tropical green, and the hills and their surrounding flat paddy lands, is one scenic aspect of this karst landscape. The Li River winds through the hills like a green silk ribbon. The town of Yangshuo itself, at the end of a 50-mi. (80-km) boat cruise from Guilin City, is one of the most picturesque centers of the area and is surrounded by karst peaks that resemble ancient Chinese hats, galloping horses, a paintbrush and a five-fingered hand. All this, packed into a small town area, has inspired the following Tang dynasty saying: "The town walls encircle less than two *li* of space, but all the houses are hidden among ten thousand hills."

To the north of Yangshuo lies Xingping, which is reputed to have "the best of Yangshuo's landscape." There, fishing rafts crisscrossing the Li River against a dramatic backdrop of hills are a typical sight. ▼ ▶

West Street

West Street (Xi Jie) is the main street in Yangshuo, an ancient town with a 1400-year history that lies along the Li River. The local residents have dubbed it the "global village" because of the numerous visitors from all over the world. Today, the mile (about 2-km) long street has over 300 restaurants, bars, internet cafes, attractive traditional-style hotels, arts-and-crafts stores and even foreign language clubs. It's an ideal place to eat and stay, and a convenient hub for touring the area. ▶

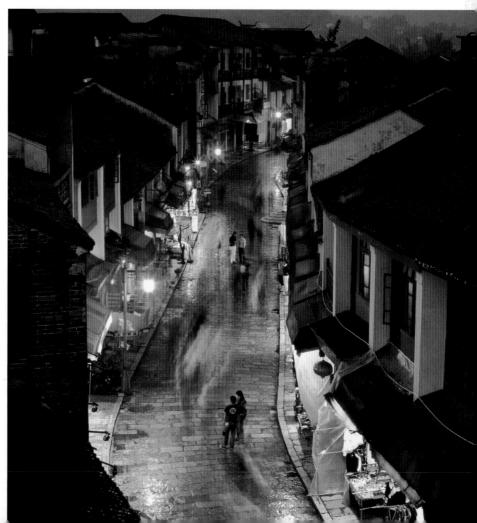

CAMEL HILL
駱駝峰

ELEPHANT TRUNK HILL
象鼻山

This limestone outcrop to the east of Guilin looks so remarkably like a camel that it is difficult to imagine it known by any other name. However, there is another similarity, and a story to go with it. The hill is sometimes called Ewer Hill because it also has the shape of a wine ewer. At its foot there is a spot called the Grave of Lei the Drinker—commemorating Lei Mingchun of the Ming dynasty who used to climb to the summit to drown his sorrows in wine, lamenting the collapse of the Ming. ▲

This is another imaginatively shaped outcrop at the confluence of Guilin's Yang and Li rivers, and the subject of a rather sad legend. It is said that the King of Heaven, taking a tour of southern China, brought with him an elephant that fell ill in Guilin. A local farmer nursed it back to health, and in return the elephant worked for him in the fields. The Heavenly King considered this a betrayal and put the poor creature to death. It promptly turned to stone. ▼

CHENGYANG WIND-RAIN BRIDGE
程陽風雨橋

Another striking example of a traditional covered bridge, this one was built by the Dong tribespeople to span the Linxi River in Sanjiang County. It was constructed in 1916 on a spot that has long been a meeting place of the Dong clans. About 250 ft. (76 m) long, it has five stone piers but otherwise is built entirely of wood. ▲

FLOWER BRIDGE (HUAQIAO)
花橋

This elegant bridge reflects the traditional Han Chinese architecture and was rebuilt in 1540 in the time of the Ming rule at the confluence of the Small East River and Lingjian River in Guilin. It is 410 ft. (125 m) long, built of rock, and actually extends way beyond the span of the river, with seven more arches besides the four that can be seen here. A green-tiled roof provides the "wind-rain" protection but is not as dramatic as those of the Dong design.

To the east of the bridge stands Hibiscus Rock, prettily named but actually a symbol of suffering: It bears the watermarks of many floods that have swept across the area in the past. ▲

GOLDEN ROOSTER HILL
金雞嶺

The Golden Rooster Hill is known for the three boulders that are positioned high above the Wu River in Lechang County. For centuries they have been seen as a roosting rooster—a fowl that, in Chinese belief and superstition, has the power to transform itself into a human being and wreak harm upon society if it so wishes. It is used in sacrifices and certainly is not eaten, its flesh regarded as unwholesome. Its crowing is said to be a sign of faithfulness, but if a hen should crow, it is taken as a sign of treachery. ▲

SEVEN-STAR CLIFFS
廣東肇慶七星岩

Rising abruptly from the northern district of Zhaoqing City in northwest Guangdong Province, these seven dramatic karst formations are arranged like the big dipper constellation and are reputed to bring together the magical forces of both the hills of Guilin and the West Lake of Hangzhou. The cliffs are also noted for the many caves at their bases, the most famous being Stone Chamber Cave, which contains an underground river accessible by boat and many inscriptions on its walls dating back as far as the 6th century. Thirty years ago a small lake under the peaks was enlarged to provide irrigation and fish-breeding grounds, landscaped and beautified and named Star Lake. Bridges and pavilions were added in the Ming and Qing architectural styles. Zhaoqing itself goes back for more than 1500 years and was formerly called Duanzhou. It is famous for its Duan ink stones and ivory carvings. ▶

DINGHU MOUNTAIN
肇慶鼎湖山

Known simply as "the lake on a hill," this scenic spot northeast of Zhaoqing is said to be where the Yellow Emperor had a large bronze cooking vessel called a ding cast and installed. The area is abundant with rare plants and also features a series of picturesque waterfalls. An old monastery called Qingyun, constructed in 1633, stands at the foot of the hill. It once accommodated about 800 monks. Two large iron woks, adequately called "thousand-people" woks, still hang in the monastery as evidence of its grander days.

▶ ▼

DANXIA MOUNTAINS
丹霞山

Sheer cliffs, rock walls, stone pillars and astonishingly shaped rocks form Danxia Mountains, the Chinese Redstone Park. Claimed to be the most unique mountain park in the southern coastal province of Guangdong, it is one of the eight Chinese geological parks or geoparks on the UNESCO's list. Danxia Mountains, meaning "red rays of the sun" in Chinese, consist of an area of 108 sq. mi. (280 sq. km) of brilliant red sandstone rocks that exemplify the landform term known as Danxia Geomorphy.

Even today many of the 680 stone hills, stonewalls and stone pillars can be viewed only from a distance. Other rock formations can be reached by precipitous steps such as the almost straight-up climb to Yangyuan Mountain and the treacherous climb up Zhanglao Peak, which provides breathtaking panoramic views of the rock formations. An easier way to see the park is via boat ride on Jingjiang River, cruising past strange and wonderful rocks, like the Sister Peak, Elephants Crossing the River and various other animal-like rock formations. Of special interest are the "male and female stones," rock formations known in Chinese as Yangyuanshi and Yingyuanshi for their startling resemblance to the male and female sex organs. ◄ ▲

ZHONGSHAN MEMORIAL HALL
中山紀念堂

This, the memorial to Guangdong Province's most famous son, Dr. Sun Yatsen, stands on the southern slope of Yuexiu Hill in Guangzhou (Canton). The republican revolutionary assumed the name Zhongshan when he was installed as interim president of China in 1922 after his initial republican movement struggled through chaos and civil unrest caused by the power play of various competing warlords.

The hall stands 161 ft. (49 m) high, and the compound occupies an area of more than 50,590 sq. ft. (4700 sq. m).

The octagonal memorial hall is palatial and has a rich color combination: vermilion columns, yellow walls and blue glazed tiles.

The hall seats over 4000 people, and there is not a single pillar to block anyone's view. Both the hall and the bronze statue of Dr. Sun Yatsen were completed in 1931 from funds raised by overseas Chinese.

This memorial hall is regarded by many as a masterpiece of modern Chinese architecture. ▲

THE ANCESTRAL TEMPLE OF
THE CHEN FAMILY

陳家祠

Built in the early 1890s from donations by members of the Chen families, the Ancestral Temple of the Chen Family, also known as the Chen Clan Academy, is situated in the old section of Guangzhou (Canton). It occupies an area of 161,500 sq. ft. (15,000 sq. m) and is the largest and best preserved and decorated Qing architecture in Guangdong Province. It was used to provide lodgings for Chen family candidates who came from all over Guangdong to prepare for the imperial examinations held in Guangzhou.

The ancestral temple has altogether 19 buildings of different sizes and is divided into four parts, centered around the rectangular 66-ft. (20-m) tall main hall, Juxian Tang (Talents Gathering Hall). The architecture is typical of traditional Guangdong style, with beautiful wall and beam decorations and legendary stories, represented in wood carvings, brick carvings, pottery carvings, stone carvings, clay sculpture and brass and cast iron. ▽ ▷

QINGHUI GARDEN

清暉園

This splendid residence, situated in Shunde County, Guangdong Province, and built in 1800, features a main house constructed in the "boat mansion" design—it looks like a traditional luxury houseboat from the outside—and is set among studios and pavilions in a water garden as fine as any found in the most celebrated center of residential architecture, Suzhou. It reflects the wealth that Guangdong and its neighboring provinces enjoyed through trade and communication with foreigners. ◄

FOSHAN ANCESTRAL TEMPLE

佛山祖廟

This temple, first built in 1085 in the Song dynasty and originally called North King, is not a place of ancestral worship at all, but it is called that because it is the oldest in Foshan City. Its main feature is a parade of beautifully sculptured ceramic figures along the ridges of its roofs, reflecting Foshan's longstanding reputation as a leading producer of porcelain and other ceramics.

The temple was rebuilt in the Ming dynasty and consists of two main halls and the Tower of Rejoicing in Immortality, Pond of Splendid Fragrance and Stage of Myriad Blessings. Nearby is a park in which stands a Qing dynasty museum. ▲

West Lake of Huizhou
惠州西湖

Lying by the side of Huizhou City in Guangdong Province, West Lake is as famous for being a supplier of freshwater fish as it is for its placid beauty. It is also associated with the famous Song dynasty poet and calligrapher Su Shi (Su Dongpo), who was banished here and became prefect of the city. During his term of office, he wrote these much quoted lines extravagantly celebrating the distinctive southern fruit, the lychee:

> *"It's spring all year round*
> *Below the Luofu Mountains. Strawberries, loquats*
> *Make their debut one by one*
> *And the lychee!*
> *O, for three hundred lychees a day.*
> *I do not mind*
> *Spending all my days south of the ranges."*

▼

Guangji Bridge

廣濟橋

Spanning the Han River in Chaozhou, this bridge looks quite modern at first glance, but its stone arches to each side of the central span reveal its true age. It was first built in the 12th century, 1690 ft. (515 m) long and constructed of granite blocks. The central span was added in the 20th century to widen its access for modern river shipping. But its traditional form remains notable as one of the four greatest ancient bridges in China. ◀

West Lake of Chaozhou

潮州西湖

In the time of the Tang dynasty, a long dyke was built in Chaozhou, separating the waters of the Han River. The enclosed area was landscaped and beautified, and today it is the city's West Lake. A popular recreation spot, it features double- and single-eaved pavilions and bridges connecting its various viewpoints and resting places. ▼

HAINAN ISLAND
海南島

ainan, off the southernmost tip of China, is the second largest of the nation's 5000 or more islands. Covering an area of 12,352 sq. mi. (32,000 sq. km), the island is low-lying in the north and mountainous in the central region and south. Its tallest hills, the Five-Fingered Mountains, reach 6165 ft. (1879 m) and are clearly visible from the mainland 11 mi. (18 km) away. Most parts of the island are idyllic—lush forests and tropical beaches being among its charms. Elsewhere, in its fertile valleys, its mixed population of native Yi and Han Chinese settlers cultivate rice, rubber, coffee, tobacco, pepper and cocoa. Mahogany is one of its most famous products, traditionally used for furniture making as far away as Suzhou. The island also has large deposits of iron ore. ▶ ▼

World's End

The somber-looking beach spot with its two huge boulders on the southern tip of Hainan Island was about as far as any Chinese official cared to go in ancient times. And even then, it meant shame to be exiled to Tianyahaijiao, literally the End of the World. It reflected the view in those days that the civilized world ended on the borders of Chinese civilization. Today, riding on the swift changes in Haikou and Sanya, the two major cities on Hainan Island that have been dubbed "China's Hawaii," this quiet beach has become one of the busiest tourist destinations. ▼

WUYI RANGE
武夷山

The Wuyi Mountains extend for 250 km through western Fujian Province. Since the Tang dynasty they have been a well-known Buddhist retreat. More than 100 monasteries have been built on their slopes and among the peaks so that the 20th-century visitor will find a wealth of ancient architecture and relics. The mountains are also renowned for their Dahongpao tea, adding to the reputation of Fujian Province itself as one of China's paramount tea-producing areas. ▲

Nine Bend Stream

Typical of the scenic beauty of much of Fujian Province is the 4.3-mi. (7-km) stretch of rugged natural parkland in the Wuyi Range, through which the river flowing from Sanbao Mountain bends and twists nine times. Every bend presents the visitor with a different view—a waterfall here, an abruptly rising peak there or an interesting rock formation.

On the left bank of the fifth bend is a studio where Zhu Xi, a famous scholar of the Song dynasty, delivered his many lectures on philosophy. Negotiating one's way down the meandering river on a bamboo raft is perhaps the most leisurely way of appreciating the breathtaking views that unfold one after another.

The Wuyi Mountains to the north of the province form the border with Jiangxi and are regarded as being among the most attractive hills in China. ▼

LUOYANG BRIDGE
福建洛陽橋

This bridge, extended by a causeway to span reclaimed land, crosses the Luoyang River between Quanzhou City and Hui'an County in Fujian Province. The bridge itself was built in 1053 and has 46 piers. First the piers of the bridge were formed in shallow water using fast-multiplying oysters as a cementing agent. Then large stone slabs were carried by boat and laid on the piers while the river tide was high.

There are 500 carved panels in the balustrades. Twenty stone lions stand guard on either side, and the structure is decorated with nine stone pagodas. The entire crossing is 1312 yd. (1200 m) long.

The bridge was reinforced with cement and steel when Quanhui highway was built in 1932, extending the width of the bridge from 5.5 yd. (5 m) to 8 yd. (7 m). ▼

MULAN DYKE
木蘭陂

Constructed in the 11th century, the now largely dilapidated dyke was once a water conservation project built to control the floodwaters and to irrigate surrounding land where the Mulan River joins Xinghua Bay in Putian, Fujian Province. ▲

STATUE OF LAOJUN
老君岩石像

This massive stone sculpture of Laojun (Laotze), the founder of Taoism, stands on the slope of Wu Mountain in the northern area of Quanzhou. It is one of very few surviving works of art in Fujian Province that date from the Song dynasty, when Chinese pictorial art and its celebration of nature reached its high point, and when, without coincidence, Taoism and its worship of man's relation to nature enjoyed an upswing too. The statue is 16 ft. (5 m) high and, naturally, is regarded as a masterpiece of the art of stonework. ◄

Kaiyuan Monastery
開元寺

Originally called the Lotus Monastery, this place of worship and meditation in Quanzhou City was first built in AD 686 in the reign of Ruizong of the Tang dynasty. Its architecture is strictly Han Chinese, yet it also points to the international contact that Fujian Province has maintained over the centuries. It features 72 panels of basrelief carved with figures of lions with human heads that is similar to the Egyptian Pharaonic style of artwork. The monastery also has columns with cornices reminiscent of classical Greek architecture. ◄

Sunshine Cliff
日光岩

Sunshine Cliff is the highest point of Longtou Shan (Dragon Head Hill) on Gulangyu (above), a small island opposite the city of Xiamen (Amoy). A monastery by the same name lies on the slopes, while nearby are well-known scenic spots hidden among huge rocks and deep caverns. On a clear day, visitors can see Jinmen across the straits. At the close of the Ming and the beginning of the Qing dynasties, the famous general Zheng Chenggong used the cliff and its environs as a training ground for his navy as part of his plan to recover Taiwan from the Portuguese. He is commemorated by a park. Some of the 17th-century relics are well preserved, such as the camp gate, and on the cliff face are carved inscriptions in bold calligraphy. ▲

HONG KONG

香港

Hong Kong has such variety packed into a small area that it amazes the visitor and tempts the Hong Kong residents to spend years exploring yet a new area of Hong Kong. The world's third largest financial center, Hong Kong's Central district rivals Manhattan for density and nonstop activity. Construction is a constant all over Hong Kong, but the business district of Central outstrips anywhere else with new, shiny towers that shoulder their shorter, older forerunners, which will soon be razed to make way for new skyscrapers. A few structures, such as the Flagstaff House (top opposite) built in 1846 as the official residence for the commander of the British forces, have survived this frantic pace, and, surprisingly, these surviving examples of old Hong Kong can be found right in the center of the city.

From Central, a short ride across Victoria Harbor on the famed Star Ferry is the Kowloon Peninsula, which includes the largest and, in parts, quite rural New Territories. The Kowloon side just across the harbor is the location for many tourist hotels and all kinds of shopping. From close to Victoria Harbor the main shopping street called Nathan Road begins with the Golden Mile that caters to visitors looking for inexpensive goods of all kinds. Nearby is the canvas-covered jade market, the Temple Street Night Market with street food, fortune-telling and Cantonese opera jam sessions in addition to bargains of all sorts. A short ride on the MTR (the HK subway system) brings locals and visitors to the adjacent Flower and Bird Market. Nathan Road continues for miles through densely packed shops and residential blocks. With enough persistence, almost anything can be found in this part of Hong Kong by the intrepid bargain hunter.

Hong Kong Electric Tram

The HK Tramways is one of the oldest public transportation systems still in operation. Inaugurated in 1904, 16 years after the Peak Tram started its service in 1888, it has provided the public with the cheapest way to travel across Hong Kong Island from Kennedy Town to Sau Kei Wan, with a branch serving the Happy Valley Racecourse. Its slow ride offers travelers a safe and leisurely way to have a firsthand look at local street life and the town. There are even open-balcony trams for tourists and private hire. While most of the trams are old-styled with slide windows, new modern trams in green and white were added to the fleet in 2000, which are more comfortable than the old ones. ▼

The Star Ferry

The Star Ferry's green-and-white boats are the oldest in the network of Hong Kong ferries. Founded in 1898, it has served as a major communication route between Hong Kong Island and Kowloon. Lovingly cared for, they also cover the shortest distance between the Central business area and the busy shopping area in Tsimshatui. While it is still commonly used as an inexpensive mode of transportation, the 10 minute Star Ferry ride offers panoramic views of the Victoria Harbor, with IFC Phase II, the Bank of China (right) and Hongkong and Shanghai Bank buildings and Central Plaza on the Hong Kong side, and the HK Cultural Center, the Peninsula Hotel and Regent Hotel on the Kowloon side. ▲

Tung Ping Chau

A visit to Tung Ping Chau provides a glimpse of Hong Kong that combines colorful history and remote island isolation. A tiny island in the New Territories that has been turned into a marine park, Tung Ping Chau was used long ago by smugglers to bring guns and opium from China. Almost deserted today, the main village on the island still has a few families, offering services to the weekend vacationers. A hike through the pleasant parklands is a good place to spot wild orchids native to the Hong Kong area. The island's footpaths will eventually lead to each end of the island, where there are large rock outcrops. At the island's south end are two huge rocks called Drum Rock, or Watchman's Tower Rock. The long thick rock (right) is part of the layer of rock that resembles a dragon's back. At its northern end, it is called Lung Luk Shui or "dragon entering the water." ▼ ▶

Po Lin (Precious Lotus) Monastery

Visitors who want to explore the outer islands in Hong Kong often make the trip to Po Lin Monastery on Hong Kong's largest island, Lantau. When first built by three monks in 1920, it only had a shrine dedicated to Buddha and was expanded over the years to become one of the top ten Buddhist monasteries in Hong Kong. The world's largest bronze Buddha (right), 100 ft. (30 m) tall and weighing 275-tons, sits on the top of the Muyu (wood fish) Peak across the monastery, truly an impressive sight for all who hike up the peak to the statue. ▼

MACAU
澳門

Macau exemplies the fascinating results of the meeting and blending of two very different cultures for nearly 450 years. A densely packed city of 450,000, where 70 percent of government revenue comes from the gambling industry today, it became the first European colony in Asia when in 1557 the Portuguese settled in the South China Sea to conduct the highly lucrative business of trade between Europe and the rest of Asia. The most advanced mapmakers and skilled sailors of Europe, the Portuguese were already old hands at this business with trading settlements in Africa and India. Macau was just the last to be founded in the string of Portuguese outposts that controlled the flow of riches from China and Japan. Happily for the Portuguese, the flow did not just go one way. The riches of Portugal's far-flung trading empire to the west brought spices, ivory, gold and highly coveted European technological inventions through this tiny settlement. ▲ ▶

The Facade of Sao Paulo

The Portuguese also brought along their specially trained missionaries. The Facade of Sao Paulo, now the only existing part of the church of Saint Paul, was the first church built in Macau in the early 17th century. The magnificent stone facade shows traces of the contributions of Portugal's Christian converts along its trading route, who were brought to Macau to help and may also have been sheltered there from the backlash against the church's activity in Asia. Sao Paulo was constructed under the direction of the Jesuit missionaries who had proselytized and gained converts to Christianity all along their route to Macau and as far north as Japan. ▲

Largo do Senado

The best way to get acquainted with Macau is through a walking tour of the historic district beginning at Largo do Senado (Senate Square). This square is paved in black and white stone tiles in a swirling wave pattern typical of Portugal. Surrounding the square are beautifully restored colonial buildings painted in delightful pastels with white, used to pick out their wonderful baroque details. It is a great place to sit and watch the doings of a community that still uses its town square for local events, socializing and meeting friends. Although the local population is mainly Chinese, the square allows the visitor to begin to recognize the Macanese in this mix. Thousands of Macanese families, often going back many generations, have mixed Chinese and Portuguese heritage. They have spanned the gap between the Portuguese and Chinese cultures for generations and created a culture uniquely their own. The most accessible feature of this unique culture is the Macanese cuisine. It combines the techniques of Chinese cooking with ingredients brought from wherever the Portuguese stopped, and from Portugal itself.

Macau also has a large number of churches, a total of 16 in a territory of barely 10 sq. mi. (26 sq. km), such as the Chapel of Our Lady of Penha on Penha Hill (right). ▼

Museum of Macau

With such a long and complicated story, Macau has done well in creating a number of museums focusing on various aspects of Macau life and history. A good place to start is the excellent Museum of Macau. Built at the base of Monte Fort, the earliest site of Portuguese occupation, the focus begins with presentations of the two cultures that lived side by side in 16th-century Macau.

As the visitor moves through the museum, the blending and cultural exchange between the Portuguese occupiers and the local Chinese provide vivid evidence of the synthesis of these two powerful cultures. ▶

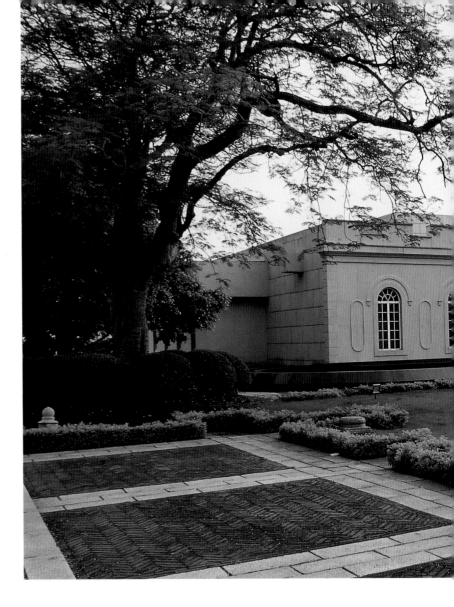

A-Ma Temple

Apart from the amazing number of churches, there are also a number of Chinese temples in Macau, the most famous being the A-Ma Temple. One of the most elaborate and the oldest building in Macau, it was built sometime during the Ming dynasty (1368–1611). It is located on a rocky outcrop just above the bay where the Portuguese first landed. The name Macau comes from the Chinese name for the bay that the A-Ma Temple overlooks. The temple is named for A-Ma, also known as Tin Hau, who is a favorite goddess of fishermen all over that area of China. ◀

322

House Museums

House Museums are even more effective at conveying the way life was lived at a certain time and place, since the rooms and their contents illustrate everything from the domestic side to leisure activities and the social status of the family that once occupied the house. The small enclave of 19th-century colonial houses on Taipa Island that have been turned into house museums is just one of the reasons to visit this island. Several of the five villas along a stretch of Taipa beach have recently been converted to allow visitors to wander through the homes as though the occupants had just left for a stroll along the sand. In addition to the museums that focus on the special aspects of the two cultures that have generated a well-established new identity, there are other museums that make Macau one of the most well-explained small cities anywhere in the world. ▼

TAIWAN

台灣

This is the largest of all of China's islands, boasting an area of 13,780 sq. mi. (35,700 sq. km). Lying just to the east off China's southern coast, it slumbered through much of the mainland's vast history, remaining relatively unnoticed beyond the sphere of Chinese affairs, and for a long time noted only for its natural resources and agricultural output. It was first colonized by the Dutch and then taken by the Japanese in the 1870s and renamed Formosa. When World War II ended in 1945, it was returned to mainland China after 50 years of Japanese occupation. When the Chinese Communists took over mainland China in 1949, the Nationalist (Kuomintang) government moved here and proclaimed Taipei its provisional capital. Although the governments on both sides of the strait have been in touch in recent years negotiating a beneficial future, the separated status remains.

Actually part of the mainland some millennia ago, Taiwan became an island when earth movements created the Taiwan Strait. Geologically it remained identifiable with the coastal regions of Fujian Province in eastern China. It is a hilly island, with a high central range running like a spine from north to south. The northern part is pockmarked with extinct volcanoes and surrounding hot springs. The highest peak, Yu Mountain, rises west of the central range to a height of nearly 13,200 ft. (4000 m). Streams are mostly short and rapid. The western part of the island is a sedimentary plain, with many beaches lining its shores. This is the main farming region of the island, supporting 40 percent of the total population. In the east and the south, the coastal plain is much narrower. Off the coast of this large island, 88 much smaller islands lie in different directions.

The tropical climate and plentiful rainfall make this region a regular producer of rice, sugarcane, tea and some 80 varieties of fruit. The forests in the hills are rich in red juniper, while camphor trees and their related produce come from the plains. There are also gold, silver, copper, coal and oil deposits. Fisheries are well developed along the shores; industries and trading are concentrated in Taibei (Taipei), the region's capital, and such towns as Jilong, Taizhong, Tainan, Gaoxiong and Taidong.

This Treasure Island of China was noted for its Eight Scenic Sights and Twelve Wonderful Spots in the Qing dynasty. The hilly regions, caverns, shoreline and lake districts create a variegated landscape, while historical sites and relics are found mainly in the old town of Tainan.

Cape Fugui

Part of Taibei (Taipei) County on the extreme northern tip of Taiwan, Cape Fugui is a transliteration of the Dutch word for promontory. A feature is its rock formations along the shores, molded into all sorts of interesting shapes by ancient volcanic eruptions and the strong seasonal northeast winds that buffet the coast. A 98-ft.- (30-m-) high eight-cornered lighthouse warns ships away from the rocky shelf. It was built in 1897. ▼

Yehliu

This, another rocky promontory 9.4 mi.(15 km) from Keelung, extends about 1.2 mi. (2 km) along the northern coast and, viewed from Keelung, looks like a turtle. It is also dotted with some 40 grotesque rock formations that look like idols erected by ancient tribespeople. Some have names that fit their shapes, such as Queen Head Rock and Resting Cow Rock. The area has been developed somewhat as a tourist venue, with bridges linking the bigger rocks. The red line shown in the picture below marks off dangerous areas where people are advised not to go. ▼ ▶

Zhinan Palace

Opulent, palatial, imperial—it is difficult to find words that fully encompass the strange grandeur of this spectacular Taoist temple in the southeastern suburbs of Taipei. Standing on a hill with its roof of yellow tiles rising solemnly into the sky against a background of dense forest vegetation, Zhinan Palace, commonly known as Fairy Temple, was built in the year 1881 (the 7th year of the Qing emperor Guangxu) and houses the shrine of Lu Dongbin, one of Chinese Taoism's Eight Immortals. Said to be a scholar and recluse who lived around 750, Lu Dongbin is the patron saint of barbers and is worshipped by the sick and disabled. His emblem is a sword, with which he conquered various forms of evil throughout the world in a vendetta said to have lasted 400 years. The temple is also dedicated to the Jade Emperor and other Taoist deities, while a statue of Lu Dongbin attracts worshippers to the nearby Silver Stream Cave, an old temple erected over a natural cave and washed by a waterfall plunging from above. ▲

Shuangxi Park

Shuangxi (Double Stream) Park, near Taipei, was landscaped and beautified to the design of the famous residential gardens of Suzhou, and so successful has the copy proved that one almost expects to see retired mandarins strolling contentedly by its waters. ◀

Longshan Temple

An old structure, first built in 1738, more than a century before the coming of the Japanese, is Lungshan Temple (opposite, bottom) southwest of Taipei. It was renovated in 1920 under Japanese supervision. The deities enshrined here include the goddess Guanyin, the Manjusri Bodhisattva, Pu Xian and 18 arhats. ◀

Sun Moon Lake

Lying in Nantou County and covering more than 3 sq. mi. (7.5 sq. km), Sun Moon Lake is the largest natural lake in Taiwan. It takes its name from its shape—the northern half is round like the sun, and the southern section is crescent-shaped. It is a popular resort, with a summer temperature of about 71.6°F (22°C) and a temperature in winter rarely falling below about 59°F (15°C). South of the lake there is a hill called Green Dragon, where several monasteries stand. One of them contains relics that are said to be those of the Tang dynasty monk Tripitaka. ▼

Ali Mountain

One of the most memorable experiences in Taiwan is traveling to the summit (or summits) of Ali Mountain to watch the sun rise over its dramatic "sea of clouds." A railway 45 mi. (72 km) long takes visitors up the mountain range, climbing from tropical to temperate forest zones and traveling through 82 tunnels, the largest of which runs for 1422 yd. (1300 m) through the hillsides. At Ali Mountain's highest peak, Ta Mountain (8531 ft. or 2600 m), visitors stand in awe of the magnificent natural spectacle of clouds hanging about 1000 ft. below them, billowing through ravines and over mountain crags and rolling in huge cotton-wool waves in from the horizon. Zhu Mountain, its smaller sister, is the best place from which to watch the sunrise, first a faint red line on the eastern horizon, then a blood-red orb lifting out of the sea of clouds and finally a series of radiant beams of light. Ali Mountain's forests produce rare high-quality timber, including Taiwan pine, China fir and Chinese juniper. In the spring, the range is full of cherry blossom. ▲

The Sacred Tree of Ali Mountain

High on Ali Mountain, central Taiwan's famous mountain stretch, stand a number of giant red Chinese junipers that are believed to be about 3000 years old. They belong to a species of trees found in Ali Mountain's virgin forests, which grow at a very slow speed. Their bark gives out a pleasant aroma. Known as the Treasure of Ali Mountain, the junipers are not only astonishingly old but also extraordinarily huge,

measuring in some cases over 160 ft. (50 m) in height and with a girth of 65 ft. (20 m). Having survived centuries of tremendous storms, forest fires and indiscriminate timber felling, they are now regarded as the god of trees. One of the junipers, which fell in 1997, was once and are honored in an inscription entitled "Ode to the Sacred Tree" carved on a stone plaque installed in a nearby wooden pavilion. ▼

Confucian Temple

This temple complex is said to have been built in 1666 in the reign of one of China's greatest imperial supporters and benefactors of the arts, Emperor Kangxi. And, as its name implies, it includes many shrines designed to commemorate the Confucian ethics of virtue, charity and duty to one's fellow man. Like Confucian temples throughout China, it has red walls, an altar to the sage, a tablet inscribed with a tribute to his "most excellent spirit" and shrines to Famous Officials, Filial Sons, the Loyal and Filial and the Virtuous.

◀

Yu Mountain

Yu, or Jade Mountain, lies in the center of Taiwan, its peaks rising to an average 6562 ft. (2000 m). However, its principal peak, named after the range, towers to 13,026 ft. (3970 m), the highest in all of eastern China. In winter, the peaks are clad in 6.5 to 9.8 ft. (2 to 3 m) of snow. As with most of Taiwan's mountain areas, Yu Mountain has its recreation areas and resorts; a path zigzags from the middle of the mountain to Paiyun Mountain Villa, a red-roofed stone guesthouse that overlooks a dramatic ravine. The path carries on from there, but the going is difficult, with sections of it actually cut into the faces of the cliffs. On its higher reaches Yu Mountain features dense forests of whitewood.

Index

Picture Credits & Acknowledgments

Front Cover: Li River. Photo by Chinese editorial.
Back Cover: from Nine Dragons Wall. Photo by Liu-Tao.
Endpapers: Nine Dragons Wall. Photo by Liu-Tao.

Panorama Stock Photos Co., Ltd.

www.quanjing.com

8-9, 10, 11, 16 (top; bottom), 17, 21, 28, 29 (bottom), 36-37, 38-39 (bottom), 41, 44-45, 46, 47, 48-49, 51 (bottom), 52, 54-55, 56, 57 (top) 58-59, 60-61 (bottom), 62-63 (top), 70-71 (top), 73 (top), 76, 77, 82, 83 (bottom), 86, 87, 89 (top), 92 (bottom), 94 (bottom), 96-97, 98, 100-101, 102, 103 (top), 105, 108 (bottom), 113, 120, 121, 124, 125, 126-127, 130-131, 134, 135, 138, 140 (bottom), 142 (top), 143 (bottom), 154-155, 156, 158 (top; bottom), 162, 163 (bottom), 164, 167 (top; bottom), 172 (bottom), 173, 174, 176-177, 178, 180-181, 184, 186-187, 188-189, 192 (top). 197 (top), 198-199, 200-201, 202, 203, 204, 208, 210, 211 (top), 213, 214, 218, 224, 226, 227 (bottom), 228-229, 236-237, 238, 240, 243, 245, 248 (top), 249, 250, 251, 252-253 (top; bottom), 255, 256-257, 258, 259, 260-261, 262 (bottom), 263, 264, 266-267, 268-269, 272 (bottom), 276-277, 280-281, 283, 300, 308, 312 (top), 312-313, 314-315, 319, 320 (bottom).

China Online Photo

www.colphoto.com

13 Gao Qin. 19 Chen Yong-Jie. 20 (top) Wang Qiong; (bottom) Jin Rui-Xiang. 22. Wang Qiong. 24 (bottom) Du Fei-Bao. 27 Zhai Dong-Feng. 30 (top; bottom) Du Fei-Bao. 31 Du Fei-Bao. 32 Zhai Dong-Feng. 33 (top) Zhang Wen-Han. 33 (bottom) Du Fei-Bao. 35 (top) Du Fei-Bao. 35 (bottom) Zhou Ju-Cheng. 37 (bottom) Liao Bin. 47 (bottom) Yin Nan. 53 (top) Xu Mei-Xia; (bottom) Xu Mei-Xia. 57 (bottom) Zhou Yong-Xiang. 64 (bottom) Yan Xiang-Qun. 65 Ding Wei-Guo. 68 Luo Xiao-Yun. 69 Ding Wei-Guo. 71 Xing Wen-Zheng. 72 (bottom) Na Ri-Song. 73 (bottom) Zhai Dong-Feng. 74 (top) Luo Xiao-Yun. 74 (bottom) Du Fei-Bao. 75 Yan Xiang-Qun. 78-79 Gao Qin. 79 Lu Qing (right). 80-81 Liu Min-Zhu. 82 Shi Xing. 83 Du Fei-Bao. 84 Luo Xiao-Yun. 85 Nie Ming. 89 Ma Zi-Xin. 90-91 Zhao Guang-Tian. 92 (top) Yang Xing-Bin. 94 Ding Ai-Guo. 99 Shao Ru-Lin. 104 (top) Qin Ling. 104 (bottom) Yin Nan. 107 Gao Ming-Yi. 114 (top) Huang Zhe-Qun. 114 (bottom) Yin Nan. 115 Du Fei-Bao. 118 Qin Ying. 122 Wu Tian-He. 128 Nie Ming. 129 Yin Nan. 132 Nie Ming. 133 (top) Yin Nan. 133 (bottom) Gao Ming-Yi. 137 Liu Qi-Yun. 152 Zhai Dong-Feng. 163 (top) Yin Nan. 165 (top) Yang Shu; (bottom) Yang Shu. 166 Yang Shu. 172 (top) Ru Sui-Chu. 175 Yin Nan. 179 Li Quan-Ju. 183 (bottom) Li Quan-Ju. 191 (bottom) Jiang Nan. 199 Du Fei-Bao. 205 Zhong Bing-Zhang. 206 Wei Qi-Yang. 207 Wei Qi-Yang. 211 Pan Guo-Ji. 215 Du Fei-Bao. 217 (top) Wang Qiong. 217 Chen Zhen-Hua. 218 Du Fei-Bao. 219 Hu Jiang-Qiao. 221 (top) Du Fei-Bao. 221 Zhang Xian-Liang. 222 Wu Jian-Guo. 223 (top) Zhang Xian-Liang. 231 (top) Yin Nan. 231 (bottom) Meng Xian-Hong. 233 Liu Hong. 239 (top) Shi Xin. 242 Zhao Bao-Wei. 244 (top) Yin Nan. 246 Bao Kun. 246-247 Bao Kun. 256 (top) Xu Mei-Xia. 262 (top) Wang Yun-Fei. 261 Tan Wei. 266 (bottom) Xu Mei-Xia. 275 Gao Ming-Yi. 291 Li Yong. 294 (top) Liu Shi-Zhao. 295 Zhong Bing-Zhang. 296 Li Ming. 297 Li Ming. 298 (top) Chen Zhao-Xing. 311 (top) Chen Hao; (bottom) Yan Xiang-Qun. 329 Wen Dan-Qing. 331 (top).

Photocome.com

www.photocome.com

15 (top) Jiang Xue; (bottom) Wu Lu-Ming. 24 (top) Li Shu-Zu. 36 (bottom) Hong Fang. 62 (bottom) Ru Sui-Chu. 72 (top) Li Quan-Ju. 72 (bottom) Li Quan-Ju. 88 Wang Mao-Huan. 111 (left) Xiao Dian-Chang; (right) Zhou Guo-Qiang. 158 Ru Shui-Chu. 182 (top) Zhang Hua; (bottom) Wu Lu-Ming. 183 (top) Li Quan-Ju. 186 Li Quan-Ju. 219 (top) Shui Xiao-Jie. 220 (top) Shui Xiao-Jie. 225 Li Quan-Ju. 225 Chai Jie. 230 (top) Wang Shun-Ling; (bottom) Wang Shun-Ling. 232 (bottom) Li Ze-Hong. 232 Li Ze-Hong 241 (top) Qin Huai; (bottom) Qin Huai. 247 Yu Hui-Tong. 248 (bottom) Wu Dong-Jun. 265 Huang Zheng-Ping. 273 (top) Li Ze-Hong. 276 (top) Wang Shun-Ling. 285 Wu Lu-Ming.

Guangzhou Integrated Image Co., Ltd.

www.fotoe.com

12 Xiao Dian-Chang. 18 Fan Jia-Shan. 34 Hu Wu-Gong. 58 Sun Jia-Bin. 64 (top) Yang Xing-Bin. 68 Li Quan-Ju. 90 (top) Hu Wu-Gong. 95. 97 Sun Jia-Bin. 115 Luo Xiao-Yun. 120 Luo Xiao-Yun. 122 Luo Xiao-Yun 136 Chen Zhan-Wu. 201 (bottom) Wei De-Zhi. 206 A Chun. 215 (bottom) Li

Ming. 220 (bottom) Yin Chun. 223 (bottom) Wang Shi-Ming. 235 Wang Shun-Ling. 270 Wang Zhi-Zhong. 271 Wang Zhi-Zhong. 274- 275 Yang Xing-Bin. 274 (bottom) Li Ming. 277 Yang Xing-Bin. 282 Liu Zi-Dian. 298 An Ge. 306 Deng Qi-Yao. 307 Huang Yi-Ming. 309 Wang Min. 324 (top) Da Zhi Image; (bottom) Da Zhi Image. 325 Da Zhi Image. 329 Da Zhi Image.

China Toursim

103 Shao Bao-Xiu. 123 (bottom) Shan Xiao-Gang. 159 Yang Bing-Zheng. 160 Yang Bing-Zheng. 161 Hu Wei-Biao. 234 Ling Jun

Others

2-3 Li Ya-Shi. 14 Zhou Zhi-Ping. 16 (bottom) Sun Chang-Shan. 23 Liu Tao. 25 (top) Li Cheng-Zhi; (bottom) Li Cheng-Zhi. 26 Li Cheng-Zhi. 27 (top) Li Cheng-Zhi; (bottom) Li Cheng-Zhi. 29 (top) Li Cheng-Zhi. 38-39 (top) Ji Jiu-Li. 40 (top) Ji Jiu-Li; (bottom) Ji Jiu-Li. 42 (top) Ji Jiu-Li; (bottom) Ji Jiu-Li. 43 Ji Jiu-Li. 45 Liu Tao. 49 (top) Liu Tao. 50 Shi Xiao-Tan. 51 (top) Shi Xiao-Tan. 60 (top) Tang Zhi-Sheng. 61 (top) Jin Ling. 66 Tang Zhi-Sheng. 70-71 (bottom) Kuang Jun. 81 (bottom) Song Kang. 84 (top) Shou Kang-Gu; (bottom) Shou Kang-Gu. 85 Shou Kang-Gu. 106 Qin Xiao-Ping. 107 (top) Qin Xiao-Ping. 110-111 Qin Xiao-Ping. 112 (top) Qin Xiao-Ping; (bottom) Qin Xiao-Ping. 116 (top) Peng Yuan; (bottom) Peng Yuan. 117 Peng Yuan. 119 (top) Peng Yuan; (bottom) Chen Hua-Li. 123 (top) Peng Yuan. 126 (top) Chang Jian-Fang. 127 (top) Chang Jian-Fang. 131 Chang Jian-Fang. 133 (top) Yue Nian; 136-137 Chen Hua-Li. 139 (top) Liu Tao; (bottom) Liu Tao. 140 (top) Liu Tao. 141 Liu Tao. 142 (bottom) Liu Tao. 143 (top) Liu Tao. 144 (top) Liu Tao; (bottom) Liu Tao. 145 (top) Liu Tao; (bottom) Liu Tao. 146 Liu Tao. 147 (top) Liu Tao; (bottom) Liu Tao. 148 Liu Tao. 149 (top) Liu Tao; (bottom) Liu Tao. 150-151 Liu Tao. 151 Liu Tao. 152 (top) Liu Tao. 153 (right) Zhai Dong-Feng. 157 Liu Tao. 168 Zhou Chang-Zheng. 168-169 Zhou Chang-Zheng. 170 (top) Zhou Chang-Zheng; (bottom) Zhou Chang-Zheng. 171 Zhou Chang-Zheng. 178 (top) Yong Cheng. 181 (top) Kuang Jun. 190 LG Chen. 192 Tang Zhi-Sheng. 193 Zhu Ming-Jian. 194 Jin Ling. 195 Jin Ling. 196 Jin Ling. 197 (bottom) Zhang Da-Ye. 211 (bottom) Shun Chi-Chin. 217 (bottom) Chen Hua-Li. 221 (bottom) Chen Hua-Li. 239 (bottom) Liu Tao. 244 (bottom) Zheng Chun-Sheng. 254 (top) Zheng Chun-Sheng. 254 (bottom) Yang He-Feng. 257 Lu Zong-Yin. 272 (top) Tang Zong-Bin. 273 (bottom) Zhu Ming-Jian. 278 (top) Tang Zong-Bin; (bottom) Tang Zong-Bin. 279 Tang Zong-Bin. 280 Luo Guang-Tai. 288 Luo Guang-Tai. 289 Zhang Jian-Yuan. 292 Li Ya-Shi. 293 (top) Zhang Jian-Yuan; (bottom) Che Shi-Ping. 294 (bottom) Li Ya-Shi. 295 (top) Che Shi-Ping. 299 (top) LG Chen; (bottom) LG Chen. 301 (top) Tom Chen; (bottom) Zhou Zhi-Ping. 302 (top) LG Chen; (bottom) LG Chen. 303 KF Loh. 304 (bottom) LG Chen. 304-305 LG Chen. 305 (bottom) LG Chen. 310 Yang Yong-Cheng. 315 (top) LG Chen. 316 (top) LG Chen; (bottom) LG Chen. 317 (top) LG Chen; (bottom) LG Chen. 318 (bottom) LG Chen. 320 (top) LG Chen. 321 (top) LG Chen; (bottom) LG Chen. 325 (bottom) Hilit. 328 (top; bottom) Hilit. 330 (bottom) Hilit

A READER'S DIGEST BOOK

U.S. Project Editor: Barbara Booth
Copy Editor: Mary Connell
Project Designers: George McKeon, Yiping Yang
Executive Editors, Trade Publishing: Dolores York, Longgen Chen, Ying Wu
Art Designers: Sally Chen, Loretta Loh
Cover Design: Sally Chen
Picture Research: Tom Chen, Willy Xu

Associate Publisher, Trade Publishing: Christopher T. Reggio

Vice President & Publisher, Trade Publishing: Harold Clarke

This book is edited and designed by Reader's Digest Association Far East Limited, in partnership with
Shanghai Literature & Art Publishing House and Shanghai Press & Publishing Development Company.

Library of Congress Cataloging-in-Publication Data

Treasures of China: an armchair journey to over 340 legendary landmarks / Reader's Digest
    p. cm.
  Includes index.
  ISBN 0-7621-0565-8
1. China–Pictorial works. 2. Historic sites–China–Pictorial works. 3. China–Antiquities–Pictorial Works.
I. Reader's Digest Association.

DS706.3.T74 2004
951'.0022'2–dc22   **2004051061**

Address any comments about *Treasures of China* to:
      The Reader's Digest Association, Inc.
      Adult Trade Publishing
      Reader's Digest Road
      Pleasantville, NY 10570-7000

For more Reader's Digest products and information, visit our website:
      www.rd.com (in the United States)

Printed in China

1 3 5 7 9 10 8 6 4 2